Grandfamilies

Grandfamilies

Stories of Children and the Loving Relatives Who Raise Them

Donna M. Butts

SHE WRITES PRESS

Published in 2026 by
She Writes Press, an imprint of The Stable Book Group

1569 Solano Ave #546
Berkeley, CA 94707
https://shewritespress.com
Library of Congress Control Number: 2026907058
ISBN: 979-8-89636-328-6
eISBN: 979-8-89636-329-3

Interior Designer: Tabitha Lahr

Printed in the United States

In loving memory of two tenacious, compassionate advocates: MaryLee Allen, whose passion for children led to meaningful child welfare reform, and Janet Sainer, who pioneered services for older adults that we take for granted today. Their work brought grandfamilies to the forefront, demonstrating how the bookend generations—our young and old—hold our civil society together. They furthered our understanding that children don't grow up in isolated pods and that older adults are as likely to be the givers of care as they are the receivers of it.

To Mary Ingraham, my aunt, who showed me how to live with an exclamation point and taught me the joy of family love and acceptance. She's a beacon of wisdom and beauty like no other.

And to the grandfamilies, whose societal contributions are as important as they are immeasurable.

GRAND Voices on Capitol Hill. Left to right: Annie Otto, Jan Wagner, Bob Ruble, Mercedes Bristol, Gail Engel, Sarah Smalls, Robert Brown (2017). Photo credit: Generations United.

Grandma's hands
Picked me up each time I fell
Grandma's hands
Boy, they really came in handy
But I don't have Grandma anymore
If I get to heaven I'll look for
Grandma's hands
—Bill Withers, "Grandma's Hands"

CONTENTS

Michelle Singletary and her grandmother, Big Mama (1991).
Courtesy of Michelle Singletary.

FOREWORD:

"Big Mama Shaped My Views About Money and Life."

by Michelle Singletary

People are often surprised when I tell them that the best financial education I ever received came from a woman who never earned more than $13,000 a year. She had no college degree, refused to invest—even in certificates of deposit—and didn't trust banks unless they were local and the tellers knew her by name. But my maternal grandmother, Marie Kelly—Big Mama to all of us—was the most disciplined, resourceful, and wise money manager I've ever known.

Big Mama didn't just raise me; she rescued me. She took in my four siblings and me when our parents could no longer care for us. Five children, all under eight, were left alone in a house without food. One day, the situation became too dangerous, and Big Mama stepped in. She brought us to her modest row house in West Baltimore and, in doing so, spared us the uncertainty of the foster care system.

Big Mama raised five of us grandkids on her small salary, a feat that still amazes me. She didn't get paid to raise us. She didn't receive any financial assistance, not because we didn't qualify but because she was too proud and too disillusioned by the child welfare system.

My grandmother symbolizes all the other grandparents who have sacrificed to provide a safe haven for their children's children.

Of course, my life story is unique to me, yet it is similar to that of the thousands of children who have been or currently are in the care of grandparents, aunts, uncles, adult siblings, or family friends.

I am part of a community of children who have been abandoned or removed from parents who are incapable of raising us.

I stand as proof of what's possible when people, connected by blood or by love, selflessly embrace the role of a parent.

One of the most influential caregivers in my life was my grandmother, Big Mama. She wasn't just a substitute parent; she was a powerful presence. Although life with her wasn't always easy, it was transformative. I am successful because of her sacrifices.

What I recall most was how my grandmother managed her money.

Big Mama was so tight with money that I swore I could hear Lincoln scream when she held a penny. I'll be honest: There were many times I questioned why God would place me in a house with a woman who was a cross between a Marine Corps drill sergeant and a guardian angel. The combination would have me praising God one day and swearing the next.

Ultimately, I realized I was meant to grow up with Big Mama. She was the savior I needed.

Big Mama inspired my financial column, "The Color of Money." Everything I know about money began with watching her stretch a modest paycheck into a life of financial stability, where every bill was not just paid on time but early. She saved because she understood that you are always one emergency away from disaster without a safety net.

She never apologized for what she couldn't provide us because she offered something more valuable: a stable life. Her financial choices weren't driven by a fear of missing out or a desire to impress; they stemmed from discipline and a strong commitment to living within her means.

People sometimes tell me I'm too strict regarding my views on money. I counter that I'm Big Mama's granddaughter.

Big Mama hated debt because she understood all too well what it could do to a person without generational wealth to rely on. She knew that one misstep—one unexpected medical bill, one job loss—could unravel everything. So, she avoided debt like the plague. She saved a portion of every paycheck and taught me to do the same.

Her fear of financial risk wasn't irrational but based on history. As a descendant of enslaved individuals, she understood how tenuous her grip on bare subsistence could be.

One of the most painful examples of that fear arose when I applied for college financial aid. I brought home a form for Big Mama to sign so I could qualify for the federal government's Pell Grant, which was awarded to low-income students. She refused to sign the form. She was terrified that the government would somehow take her house. At the time, I was devastated. I didn't understand; I just wanted to go to college. But looking back, I see how deeply rooted that fear was. The house wasn't just shelter; it was part of her retirement safety net and legacy.

Thankfully, I received a full academic scholarship to the University of Maryland, College Park, so she didn't have to fill out that financial aid form.

Despite her fear, Big Mama had incredible financial wisdom. Because of her, I have always had several dedicated savings accounts.

"Every penny ought to have a purpose," she would say.

Many of the columns I write or workshops I've led on budgeting, saving, or avoiding debt can be traced back to my grandmother's lessons on managing money.

I now realize that what she provided was more than just financial advice. She used her money lessons to teach me resilience and resourcefulness.

I'm honored to serve on the board of Generations United and be part of a mission that emphasizes the needs of many grandparents, many of whom are retired or nearing retirement, who suddenly find themselves raising children again. They do so out of love. However, love alone doesn't cover the costs of diapers, school supplies, or college tuition. These families need support, not just financial but also emotional, legal, and logistical.

Generations United provides advocacy and resources to ensure these families are not overlooked.

I know what it means to be a child in a kinship household, and this motivates me to carry that legacy forward.

Big Mama didn't live long enough to see me become a personal finance columnist. But whenever someone writes to say, "Your column changed the way I handle my money," I know who deserves the credit.

Like many other grandparents, Big Mama gave me more than just a roof over my head; she gave me a solid foundation.

I am grateful to her and for Generations United and its mission of supporting grandparents who, for various reasons, have become anchors in their grandchildren's lives while shaping who they will ultimately become.

"I Vote!"

GRAND Voice: Adrian Charniak

My grandson Joey came into our lives on June 11, 1998, and there weren't many easy days at first. The Illinois Department of Children and Family Services was involved from the beginning. His mother abused drugs; he was born with cocaine in his system. Because of my son's chronic illness, my husband and I were told that we'd be able to take the child. But when the time came, Joey was given to his mother.

They had an apartment down the block, and she would come and go. At one point, she packed her stuff and took Joey with her. From October to February. I sat back, praying that we'd find them.

Eventually, she and my son divorced, and my husband and I got court orders to get Joey back. We brought the papers to his other grandmother's house, where he and his mother were supposed to be—but they weren't. Eventually the police called and said that they saw his mother in Stickney, two towns over from us, putting Joey in the car.

My brother and his girlfriend, Shirley, went over with the police department to get him. When they came back, Shirley had Joey under her coat. It was the dead of winter, and he had no jacket on—just a onesie and a soaked diaper.

After my son died and Joey was going on eleven, his mother tried to get him back again. The court told us that she had to have visitation rights.

Thank God we had the love and the strength from each other to carry us through this. And hundreds of police reports—hundreds. The police department knew us already; it was terrible. And plus, Ron and I had to give Joey's mother support, seventy dollars a week.

After one visit, Joey came home and said, "I can't go back there again. The word 'A-S-S' is spray-painted on the front room wall." If he lived there, he would have to sleep in the basement, he said. "The toilets were out in the open, with no doors, no nothing. I can't go there."

He had two friends who lived behind us, Packy and Patrick, and their parents were with us 100 percent. There was a crawl space in their house, and the kids put a cot in there, blankets and water, a cooler, candy, chips, cookies—you name it. If Joey had to go with his mother, he was to run over to Packy's house, go into the crawl space, and the kids would cover it up with their door so they couldn't find him.

I worked for an orthodontist for thirty-seven years, and he was very supportive. One of our patients was a judge, and when she came into the office one day, my boss said, "Go and tell her what's going on."

I said, "No, I can't do that. I don't think it's right."

He said, "Adrian, you want something done? You go talk to her."

I told her we were before a judge who kept giving Joey's mother more visitation. We went back seven times, but the judge was not listening. Well, the judge who was our patient said, "Adrian, I think you've got the backbone and the balls to do this."

I asked, "What's that?"

She said, "You're going to tell him you're a United States citizen, you vote. And his name's on the ballot."

We went back to court with our big stack of papers, but he was still not listening. I put my hand up, and Ron goes, "Adrian, we're going to get thrown out."

I said, "That's okay, because then I'll go out screaming and run, and then somebody will hear me."

"Excuse me, sir," I said to the judge.

"What?" the judge asked.

I said, "I'm a United States citizen. I vote. Your name's on the ballot." I just blurted it out. I could feel our patient holding me there and telling me, "This is what you need to say."

The judge pushed back his chair, put his hands on his head, and said, "Gram, tell me everything."

"Well, there were the times when Joey brought live bullets home," I began. I showed him all the documents, everything.

He looked at them, and he said, "No visitation, unless Grandma and Grandpa say it's okay."

Thank you, God, *I thought. It was a nightmare, but we survived.*

I think everything that has happened has given us more strength to fight. I tell other grandparents: Hey, you know, if we did it, you can do it too.

Don't let it get you down, I tell them. Whatever baloney is being dished out to you, you're going to get the strength to get that steak eventually.

INTRODUCTION:

You Don't Age Out of a Family

I don't have children or grandchildren. No one in my immediate family has had to raise a grandchild, niece, or nephew. I wasn't aware of the needs of grandfamilies, as we call them—families like Adrian Charniak's—until, in 1997, I joined a tiny new nonprofit called Generations United.

In the many years since then, I've come face-to-face with thousands of families in which a grandparent or another close relative or family friend has said yes to caring for a child.

I was not unique in my lack of awareness. At the time, many of the other advocates, researchers, and professionals who've since worked diligently to build awareness and change policy and public perceptions about the families didn't have a personal tie to the issue. But as one colleague said, "You meet them, and they find their way into your heart."

I first heard Adrian's story when she spoke at an event at the National Press Club in Washington, DC, which was designed to bring attention to grandfamilies' experiences. The diminutive, gray-haired Czechoslovakian from the Chicago suburbs was shy—not used to being in front of people unless she was singing in her church choir. I watched as she took a deep breath and quietly told the crowd her story.

Adrian ended with an illustration that inspires me to this day. She said that while most of her friends boasted about golfing or planning cruises to exotic places, she cruised too—to carpool lines, skateboard parks, and pediatrician appointments. She arranged her life around the needs and schedule of her grandson, Joey.

Adrian became Joey's primary caregiver when she was in her mid-fifties and supporting an ailing husband and aging mother. Raising her grandson without a formalized relationship such as adoption, legal custody, or guardianship, she had to fight for the recognition, resources, and services Joey needed. Fight she did, appearing in court 127 times, racking up more than $100,000 in legal fees, and exhausting her pension.

"You did it, Gram," said one of the sheriff's deputies in the back of the courtroom, as she and Joey walked out for the last time. "You did it."

Adrian Charniak's Family

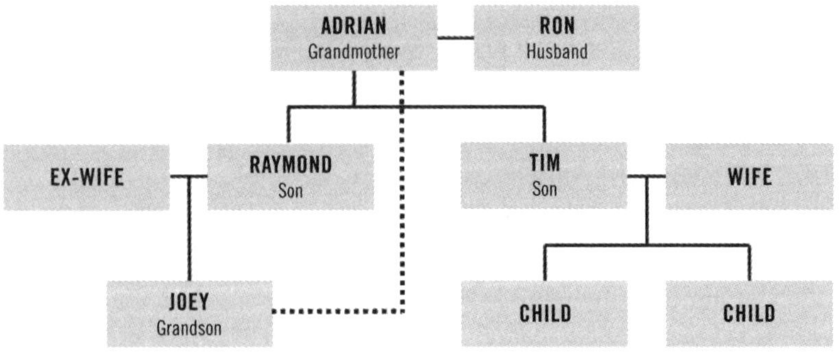

Today, in the United States, more than 2.4 million children live in grandfamilies like Adrian's.[1] Until recently, their experiences have been all but invisible. If they were in the public eye, they were portrayed as "broken," perpetuating intergenerational cycles of poverty and raising children only for the money provided by the state or federal government to do so.

Often, that is the starting point: a loss, a lack.

This is not that story.

In all the time that I have served as the executive director of Generations United, I've never met a grandparent or aunt or uncle who said they wouldn't take their grandchild, niece, or nephew in if faced with the choice of caring for the child or turning them over to the custody of the child welfare system, to be raised by people they don't know in foster homes.

Grandfamilies is the story of a crucial choice made by relatives of all ages and backgrounds who rise to this most essential of occasions and navigate the challenges that come along.

In the foreword, *Washington Post* columnist Michelle Singletary talks about being "part of a community of children who have been abandoned or removed from parents who are incapable of raising us." While some people may view children whose parents cannot care for them as a bundle of problems to be solved, these caregivers believe as Adrian does when she says, "We don't make garbage; these kids are good." They know that a child ages out of a system but never ages out of a family.

Grandfamilies take in kids, often more than one brother and sister at a time, and keep them together and connected to their roots, culture, and tribe. They fight systems that abandon them, telling them that their families don't fit their guidelines, so they can't serve them. They do time in waiting rooms and court hearings. They put themselves at financial risk and sacrifice their own health—all with the dream of making a better life for the children they love. Rather than being lost in a system, the children know every day that they are more than a case file.

"Other people don't realize how hard it is," one grandparent told me. "Or how gratifying."

This is also the story of how decades of blood, sweat, tears, and incremental wins have changed the conversation and the lives of grandfamilies. For nearly thirty years, we at Generations United have advocated for policies that support the needs of both the children and the adults raising them. Together with our national partners, we continue to address the policy gaps, lack of recognition, and misperceptions that can make the tough job of raising children even harder. We do it by making sure that the voices of grandfamilies are included in policy and other discussions: Nothing about us without us.

Some of the people you'll meet in the following pages are well-known figures in politics, entertainment, and media. "My grandmother . . . taught me about hard work," said then-candidate Barack Obama in 2008, as he accepted his party's nomination. "She's the one who put off buying a new car or a new dress for herself so that I could have a better life. She poured everything she had into me. And although she can no longer travel, I know that she's watching tonight and that tonight is her night, as well."

President Obama was far from the first commander in chief who was part of a grandfamily. That recognition goes to President George Washington and his wife, Martha, who raised her grandchildren at Mount Vernon. They built the democracy we all know alongside other early leaders in our country's revolution—including John Hancock, who was raised by his uncle.

Some of the relative caregivers and their children whom you'll encounter here are not household names. Many are key parts of our GRAND Voices Network, who have stepped into power as leaders and advocates, and some of the young people they raised have become caregivers themselves. They represent every generation, socioeconomic status, and corner of the nation. The experiences they share reflect the myriad complexities grandparents, other relatives, and close family friends face when rallying to raise children whose parents are unable to do so.

Caregivers do not automatically hold legal rights, as grandfamilies often form without advance planning. This limits the ways they're able to navigate the education and health-care systems on behalf of the child in their care. Federal, state, and local policymakers have only within the past few decades begun to recognize these families and act to reduce barriers.

As most relative caregivers are raising children outside of the child welfare system, their families are ineligible for certain essential funding and services. Even if some policies have shifted to support relative caregivers without a formal, legal relationship, the families may not be aware of their options.

The pages that follow chart the evolution of the grandfamilies movement, highlighting essential wins that often began with a caregiver's decision to share their family's story. I join their calls for action at the community, state, and national levels, echoing Adrian, who, now well into her eighties, is still on the front lines of a movement to secure a better future for families like hers. "Each rally makes me realize what my job on Earth is," she told me. "It is to keep helping others in our situation."

"I Never Got a Manual."

GRAND Voice: Bob Ruble

When I started this, I wasn't old enough to be a grandfather, but I'm up to that age now where I could be considered one. I always had to say "uncle," though the grandfamily community has become more inclusive now. I never got a manual when I brought my niece home. Still, she just turned thirty and has graduated from college, so I think we're doing okay.

The very first time I went to a support group meeting, I was having difficulties. She was getting to that lovely age of twelve or thirteen, and all hell had broken loose. I couldn't tell you how many times I'd just thrown up my hands and gone into my room. But this is what's amazing to me about the mind of a teenage girl: One minute she is angry and arguing with me. She goes into her room, slams her door. (I've learned not to follow her.) And then I hear her coming down the hallway, saying, "Hey, which shoes look good with this dress?"

I needed help.

When I walked in, I thought I was at the wrong meeting. I was the only man and, I say this jokingly, the only person in there who didn't have gray hair. It was the epitome of grandparents there, you know. Still, as I learned to mix with other people, I learned that anybody could do it: An uncle could do the job of raising a girl as a single parent—I could do all that.

Now, at meetings, before a conversation gets going, I kind of establish myself as a guy chatting among all these women: "I raised my niece since she was eight. She just turned thirty." I can say it as quickly as that—say that I'm a single parent, so that people understand that I'm not just some weird guy who's in this thing looking for grandmas who raise children.

My sister struggled with substance abuse for years. When she became pregnant, I worried that it was not going to work, but I hoped for the best. My niece was taken into custody a couple times. Once, they were in a motel, and my sister passed out. Her little six-year-old girl ran down across the parking lot, banging on the night window, saying she can't wake her mother up.

I was married at the time. I was an electrical contractor; my wife was working for an airline. We were traveling the world. We never had any biological children ourselves. For a while, with my niece, my thought process was, I don't want to look, because if I look, I'm gonna get involved. But I did keep my eye on it. I would call Child Protective Services. I couldn't say that she was actually being abused. I just said the situation was really bad.

One day I went into the bedroom where they both slept. I pulled the sheet back on the bed, found two loaded needles, and immediately called the police. Obviously, they arrested my sister—child endangerment, all the great things to go with it. My niece comes running down the street, crying, "Mom, Mom!" The police made the decision to take my niece into custody because they had been in the house.

The county had jurisdiction of her, and she was what they call "placed"—which is really a bad word, "placement"—in a group home. A safe place, but really a terrible place to be as a child. And this was her third time.

The next day I got a phone call, which happens to a lot of people. "Hey, you know, we have your niece here. You are the only one that we can immediately entrust her with, and you need to make a decision in about five minutes . . ." At least that's how it sounded to me.

Once we brought her home to live with us, we called around, trying to find out how to get her to a doctor. She had no clothes, so we went out to get appropriate clothing. We tried to get her into her room, but she couldn't sleep in a bed. She had to sleep on the floor. My wife slept in the room with her.

The next day, a guy came to our house, knocking at my door, saying, "We're here to see Kindra." And I'm like, Who the hell are you? They checked everything, made sure we didn't have bombs lying around and stuff, and gave us a piece of paper that we signed.

Once we initially got her settled, we had to get her into school. I decided to move her to a school near me, where she was identified as gifted and talented. The problem was that the school in my school district was about six months ahead, curriculum-wise, of the school that she'd left. We had to catch up big-time. I immediately bought her math textbook. Found it on eBay. I would stay ahead a day, a lesson a day.

We continued this way until we got to about her first and second year of high school, when I said, "Wow, this is too much for me. I can't stay ahead of it." I did well in math, but the way it is now is really accelerated. She worked hard, and we found tutoring help.

When they're in high school, you're part of their education. It's no longer you get a report card and go talk to the teacher. No, *you've got to be right there, monitoring. You've got to be engaged every step of the way. That was a learning experience.*

My wife and I separated. I was scared to death, because, you know, I'm a single man. I have an almost nine-year-old girl; what kind of suspicion is that going to open up? You know, just a big target on my back.

A lot of bumpy stuff happened along the way, and we got through it. As she got older, I had two goals. One was to get her through high school. She'd be eighteen one month after high school graduation. The other was to make sure she didn't get pregnant or arrested. In high school, the influences are there. You try to do everything that you can, so that you get the child to the other side and everybody survives.

I'd always taken her to a pediatrician, but obviously, she got to a certain age, and I had to start sitting in the hallway. I called it the penalty box. I'll never forget when she was twelve, and the pediatrician said, "Well, you know, I'm going to ask Uncle Bobby to stand out in the hallway."

My niece said, "Are you gonna ask me if I'm having sex or doing drugs?" That's what she said. Right in front of me. She said, "No, I'm not having sex. I'm not doing drugs."

I said, "Okay, I'm gonna go out now."

She's an open book, you know: "Hey, I'm at school, and I have a really bad period, and I have cramps." She could tell me that, no problem. When she began to develop, I took her to Victoria's Secret, and I said, "Hook her up." I sat there, and three hundred bucks later, I was out the door with four bras.

I'd say to anybody who's a caregiver raising a relative to stick with it, get the help that you need, learn, because you're going to make mistakes. Believe me, I made a lot of mistakes.

I came to the relative caregiver community by looking for help, and then I started looking for ways to help. I found myself speaking at the county level, then the state level. I went to a GrandRally in 2017 and met so many people wanting to see true change in how these children are handled and the support they get. Because these children have absolutely no choice, right? They were born into this, and they can't pick their parents.

Hopefully, when they become parents, it will just slowly put social workers out of a job. That would be fine with me.

CHAPTER ONE:

Challenging Stereotypes: What Is a Grandfamily?

"Family doesn't have to be blood. It really comes down to the relationships you can have. Whoever loves you, and you love, is your family."
—Chad Dingle, grandson, Oregon

In every family, the fates of the generations are intertwined. This is uniquely true for families where a grandparent or another close relative or family friend is raising a child.

In most cultures, there is a word for the idea, and the ideal, of family—that extended network of loved ones to envelop you in times of celebration and need.

Ohana in native Hawaiian. *Familia* in Spanish. *Sidanelv* in Cherokee. *Mishpachah* in Yiddish. *Kin* in Old English. Whatever your tradition may call this network, the word is a sign that all of us, in our own ways, are driven to care for one another.

When people think of an adult in midlife stepping into a caregiving role, they're likely to assume that it will be for a parent or a spouse. The federal government has defined family caregiving in this way since the 1970s. But millions of grandparents and other close relatives or family friends are raising children with or without legal custody or guardianship. For every child in foster care, an estimated nineteen are being raised by relatives, predominately grandparents, outside that system.[1]

Grandfamilies may come together by need, but they stay together by choice. Throughout history, grandparents—grandmothers in particular—who are the carriers of culture and knowledge have also been the protectors of the vulnerable young. In stories from every corner of the world, elder women cared for the children while a more able generation went to hunt and gather or sow and reap. Today, parents are more likely to commute to work or log on from a home office, but the grandparents are still there, providing children with an essential continuity of love and support until a parent can step back into the role of caregiver.

This care is not exclusive to grandparents, however. Families and communities of all kinds receive and give care as they are able, with the expectation that the younger generation will be better prepared to do the same. This social compact between generations is how families and societies have flourished throughout history, and it is ever more essential today. As the late anthropologist Margaret Mead once said, "Nobody has ever before asked the nuclear family to live all by itself in a box the way we do . . . with no relatives, no support, we've put it in an impossible situation."[2]

The concept of community care—the reliance on others, the responsibility to give—is foundational for families at every stage of their lives. Many of us have experienced or observed care extending beyond what is considered a "typical" family dynamic.

In the remote desert of northern Namibia, the Himba children are exclusively breastfed. A University of California,

Los Angeles, anthropologist found that the mothers did not have struggles with breastfeeding that can be common with new mothers. Part of the reason for the new mothers' success, researchers believe, is that they've been exposed to breastfeeding since childhood.[3]

Himba mothers, who deliver at home, have uninterrupted contact with their babies from birth. The elder women of the tribe teach the young mothers how to breastfeed by example; they show them how to safely carry their infants on their backs while working in the fields, so that they can continue feeding the children. Since childhood, they've been shown how to mother. They're not on their own, trying to figure it out.

Collective, multigenerational care has many documented benefits—and it's increasingly common in the United States. Here, one in four of us live in a household with three or more generations. Many families do so for financial reasons, but another key motivating factor is the need for childcare and elder care. These experiences cut across racial, ethnic, and geographical lines. Black, American Indian, and Alaska Native (AI/AN) children and caregivers are more likely to be part of grandfamilies than the general population—likely a result of communities' cultural strengths, as well as of institutional racism, implicit bias, and poverty.[4]

While every grandfamily is unique, at the heart of each of their stories is that vital decision reflecting loyalty, love, and commitment, often against tough odds. In many grandfamilies, caregivers choose children who, sadly, have been abandoned, neglected, harmed, or forgotten by their parents. If not for the relatives, the children might be caught in a vicious cycle of poverty, living on the streets or in prison, or worse.

Not all children in grandfamilies have been abandoned. Sometimes people may be temporarily unable to parent, as is the case during military deployments or time away in a treatment program. The picture that many relative caregivers step into includes the child's parents.

"My parents were too young to be parents," said Lance Robertson, who served as assistant secretary for aging and the administrator of the Administration for Community Living (ACL) during President Donald Trump's first term. "They could have raised me, but my grandpa said, 'Let's be logical.' He understood [that] he and my grandmother would be providing the resources and be the role models for me, so it was easier to be under their roof. My parents were always in my life and to this day are my best friends."

Generations United has from the beginning understood that a grandfamily's story is a complex, multigenerational one. It's about both a child *and* the caring adult who steps up to help.

Historically, advocacy groups and researchers looked at families' needs from their unique age lenses. The needs of children living without their parents were addressed through the child welfare system. The needs of older adults were addressed by the Administration on Aging. The challenges weren't considered holistically, from an intergenerational family perspective.

When leaders at the National Council on Aging, Child Welfare League of America, Children's Defense Fund, and AARP founded Generations United in 1986, there was no agreed-upon definition of a family formed by a relative caregiver and only estimates on the number of these families. One state used three different definitions for this type of family.

This began to change in 2000, when the US Census included a question about grandparent-headed households that Generations United helped shape. There is still confusion, as some groups use different sources and numbers.

Lance Robertson with his grandfather, Papa (1976). Courtesy of Lance Robertson.

"We got relative placement—a term used in 1993," said Victoria Gray, an Arizona-based caregiver and advocate, who gained custody of her four-month-old granddaughter in February 1993. "The current kinship and grandfamily just didn't exist at that time."

Back then, when a child came into the child welfare system, there was no mandate to try to find family members to take in the children. Everything that gives children a strong foundation was ignored. Sibling groups were often ripped apart and put into different foster homes. Race and ethnicity weren't considered, which meant children were often separated from their family roots and cultural traditions. Families searching for support often hit a dead end.

"She came with one bottle, a diaper bag with a few diapers, and we were given phone numbers to call for assistance," said Victoria. "We called the first number, and it was disconnected. We called the second number and left a message. No one ever called us back. On the third number, we got someone who said, 'I don't know why they gave you our number. We don't do that service.'"

Janet Sainer, the former head of New York City's Department for the Aging, brought the needs of relative caregivers to the White House in 1995. Serving as a special consultant to the Brookdale Foundation, Janet helped to establish the Relatives as Parents Program (RAPP), which would go on to fund the development of grandparent support groups throughout the country.

She did so by reaching out to Bob Blancato, the newly appointed executive director of the 1995 White House Conference on Aging—a once-in-a-decade convening focused on issues and public policies relevant to older Americans. Janet told Bob that older relatives raising children was the largely ignored, emerging aging issue of the next decade. Then she began drafting a resolution to address it.

President Bill Clinton and Bob Blancato following his appointment to head the White House Conference on Aging (1995). Courtesy of Bob Blancato.

Thanks to Janet and Bob's foresight, the White House Conference on Aging's report included three recommendations: ensure caregiver access to public benefits and services, grant legal custody or guardianship to grandparent caregivers, and educate professionals and lay people about the needs of grandparent caregivers.

This was the moment when Generations United became the glue that would bring and hold together people and groups working on behalf of relative caregivers. Together with our national partners, we began a journey to address the policy gaps, lack of recognition, and misperceptions that made the tough job of raising these children even harder. We did it by making sure the voices of grandfamilies were included in policy discussions about child welfare reform, aging services, housing policy, and more.

Understanding the challenges through a range of perspectives is especially important, as no two grandfamilies are alike. Many caregivers don't see themselves in the words "parent" and "grandparent"—and never will. While grandparents over age sixty comprise many relatives raising children in the United States, Generations United's network also includes the crucial voices of brothers and sisters, aunts and uncles, cousins, and close friends who, from age eighteen on up, have stepped into a caregiver role at a time of need.

The Origin of "Grandfamilies"

There have long been myths and stereotypes surrounding households where a child is raised by a loved one other than their parents. The image of an inner-city, low-income, single Black grandma became a popular, though seldom accurate, representation of a relationship that exists in every culture, income bracket, city, and state.

One egregious, bold-faced newspaper headline called these caregivers "Country Club Grandmothers," implying they were only taking in the children to be able to get their hands on the child-only, Temporary Assistance for Needy Families (TANF) grant. That article mentioned grandparents received $161 per month for raising a child in this "lucrative" deal. It didn't, however, reference the $165,630 that reportedly was needed to raise a child to the age of seventeen in 2000—which was, at the time, about $812 per month.[5]

If grandparents were doing it for the money, they got the short end of the stick.

At the time, some conservative lawmakers' arguments against support for these families often wound back around to "the apple doesn't fall far from the tree." Their flawed logic: Why should taxpayers support raising another generation of damaged children perpetuating the cycle of intergenerational poverty?

Another popular argument: "Grandparents have always raised grandkids, and in my day, they bucked up and did it on their own. Why should we give them money when they're doing what they should be doing?"

In 2005, Generations United led an effort to challenge stereotypes and create a shared understanding of these families' strengths and challenges. With funding from Pew Charitable Trusts, we enlisted strategists Margaret Mark and Marvin Waldman to help change the labels and framing.

"When we first started our research, virtually no one had awareness of the problems faced by those who came to be known as grandfamilies. And that includes me," said Marvin. "But what was amazing [was that] as soon as the problem was explained, it clicked. People understood it, people empathized with it, people wanted something done about it, which made our job easy. All we had to do is find the right words."

We found that people were most moved by the innocence of the children and the moral strength and sacrifice of their caregivers. To tell the whole story, we needed terminology that felt more compassionate, inclusive, and expansive.

People preferred terms that emphasized keeping families together. They chose "fund" over "subsidy" because the former felt more dignified and less value laden.

The focus groups debated labels like "kinship care," which every participant except one, a social worker, disliked. (They said it sounded "cold," and like a "social work term.") The labels that resonated almost universally were "families raising families," "stay together families," and "grandfamilies."

The term "grandfamilies" was in use by a housing project in Boston. When we told them that advocates wanted to use it, they didn't object. While no single term works for every family, and we support each relative caregiver's individual preferences, "grandfamilies" has proven to be effective for us and for the families themselves. "I live in a grandfamily" sounds so much better to a child on a playground than "I'm in kinship care."

Designed to be inclusive of all groups, the term "grand" has become a way to honor the caregivers and the children in their care. It represents the ways in which the timeless concept of family care is ever evolving to meet the moment. Advocacy work on behalf of grandfamilies must do the same.

As we look to the future, we celebrate our successes: In September 2023, for example, a new federal regulation was finalized that allows states, tribes, and territories to create foster care approval standards tailored to relatives. This means that children can be cared for by the people they know and love even if their home doesn't meet traditional foster care requirements.

If this had been the case in 2001, when JJ Hitch's retired grandparents took him in, along with his three siblings, life would have been much different. They wouldn't have had to declare bankruptcy to complete an extensive home remodeling project that would provide each child with their own bedroom just to meet foster care licensing requirements.

Loved ones who step up to raise children in need are very much a part of our American way of life—and they need to be acknowledged and supported fairly. While a term like "grandfamily" may be somewhat new, and their origin stories can be complex, we can all understand a family's challenges and hopes for the future.

"People Are Looking for Answers."

GRAND Voice: Robert Brown

On May 21, 2006, my mother-in-law, my father-in-law, my wife's aunt, my wife's cousin, and my daughter were killed at a church shooting in Baton Rouge, Louisiana. My wife was shot in the back of the head, and she survived. My daughter had three sons. Her estranged husband was the one who committed the crime.

Three sons. Five and a half, two and a half, and eight months old. My wife and I raised them. Now they are twenty-three, twenty, and eighteen.

I won't say there haven't been challenges. There are always challenges. We were raising children whose parents were gone, and they didn't have anywhere else to go.

While the young man was in prison, awaiting trial, he told his mother and sister that he was trying to hire a hit man to take my wife out, so she wouldn't testify against him. For three weeks, my wife had to stay in the house twenty-four hours a day. When the judge came back on the bench, the SWAT team came to my house, and they put us in a big black van with black windows that I'm sure were bulletproof. They took us downtown, my wife gave a deposition, and then the judge said that because of our situation, our family needed to get out of town.

There were no safe havens then. So, while we were still paying for our house in Baton Rouge, we wound up staying in Atlanta, Georgia, for eight months.

By this time, my wife had left her job, and I was close to retirement. We had to rent a three-bedroom apartment in Atlanta that was close to $2,000 a month, while keeping our house note and all the utilities going in Baton Rouge. When we returned, I had to get a bigger house because I needed a room for everybody. We were feeding three children . . . just think of the expenses. We used a lot of retirement funds this way.

Grief affects different people differently. About six months after the trial was over, my mother had a massive heart attack, and she died. Three months later, my sister-in-law died of a stroke. She was forty-seven.

My son was born the same day as his sister who was killed—the same birthday, four years apart. After the shooting, he had to go make funeral arrangements while I was up at the hospital with my wife. He was in the business world; he knew exactly what to do. But, you know, he never stopped grieving. He passed away at thirty-four years old.

No matter what level of life we're at, we all have some sort of issue. When things happen, especially a tragedy, something that's minor going on with somebody can be elevated to another level. That's why mental health is very important.

Coca-Cola, my employer, said that they would pay for three sessions with a psychiatrist for anyone connected with me: me, my wife, my daughter, my son . . . It could be my in-laws—anyone who had been in pain. It was very, very helpful.

The sheriff's deputy told us about this organization, Baton Rouge Crisis Intervention Center, where psychologists could help young kids deal with grief. On Mondays, they would have a group for the kids, and the parents would have a session together too. I think the boys went through that for about five years.

I was seeing the same psychologist. Her name was Dr. Norton, and she was a nice little lady. The way she treated these boys—she was like another grandma. When the trial was going on, she made sure she was down there with us.

I tell people: There are resources out there. If you can't think of anybody, if you don't know where to go, call the fire department. Call the sheriff or the mayor's office and they can direct you. Just get somebody to connect you with something.

During that trial, the father's rights were not terminated. It took us twelve years to adopt the kids. Every time we tried, he came up with something.

A friend of my wife's told her that there was a Grandparents Raising Grandchildren conference in Baton Rouge every year. We went, and they had all kinds of literature and resources that people can use. One of the guest speakers was this young lawyer—a real nice guy. After, they had a meet and greet, and we were introduced to him. We explained our situation.

"I can get that done for you," he said.

It took this attorney a couple of years to get the adoption settled, and this young man who had committed the crimes was still pursuing the matter through the family courts—still handwriting stuff and sending it. Finally, we got them adopted.

Some people who have lost a loved one and have to care for grandchildren think that it's going to be the end of the world. Generations United has a way of letting people know it's not—that there are resources out there that can help. They are providing a platform for people to be able to speak out, to be able to say what they are going through, what they went through.

As a part of the GRAND Voices national advocacy group, I go to Capitol Hill because I want Congress to know what's going on out there. They need to know that people are looking for answers. I'm *looking for answers.*

When you have their attention, when you say it like that, then you go ahead and tell your story. You know, I want things to get better. I want people to be in the know of how a tragedy came into my life.

I share my story because people want to hear from somebody that went through something. That way, they can say, "Oh, well, I'm not the only one."

CHAPTER TWO:

Unplanned, by Default, and in a Crisis: The Birth of a Caregiver

> "Who do you call when you're the one who everyone calls?"
> —Santana, aunt, Wisconsin[1]

On a typical bright fall Monday morning in the working-class Chicago suburb of Berwyn, the Gift of Hope Grandparent Support Group chatted away over coffee and pizza. Then Adrian Charniak called the meeting to order, reminding them of some of the national and state organizations that she had found so helpful along her journey to get custody of and raise her grandson. This included Greenlight Family Services, which provided free legal services when her pension ran out and the court hearings kept coming.

After the announcements, she introduced an elder fraud expert from the State Attorney General's office, who had joined them to share the latest swindles. "You ever heard of the romance/sweetheart scam?" the representative asked.

"Medicaid open enrollment scam?"

"Home repair scam?"

Heads nodded as she gave each example. Then she turned to a growing type of fraud—grandparent scams.

The nodding intensified as the specialist described in detail frantic "grandchildren" calling to say that they were in trouble and needed money. Adrian told the group that she always answers the phone because it might be a grandparent in need. If it's not, and the phone solicitor asks her how she is, she answers by saying that she's busy having sex and hangs up. But one time, she said, she couldn't help herself: She baited the caller.

The man began in an anxious voice, Adrian said. "'Grandma, I've been in a car accident, and I need your help.'" She played along, drawing him out as he told her about the accident and how much money he needed her to send him in cash. When she tired of listening, she said, "You should be ashamed of yourself. You aren't my grandson, and if you were, you'd know no one calls me Grandma." And with that, the woman known only as Babi hung up.

Like Adrian, many relatives who step in to raise children later in life have finely tuned street smarts and survival skills. They've been honed over many years of challenges and often a lot of pain. They come to a support group searching for answers, often at someone else's suggestion, but they also have wisdom to offer. The camaraderie found in community is not only about referrals to resources and services; it's also about a shared way of life.

The speaker answered the group's questions and closed with a prepared speech. Then she stopped.

She was so glad she knew about the group, she said, adding that she would be back. Her niece had come to live with her for "two weeks" two months ago, and she didn't see an end in sight. Now she knew what they had become—a new grandfamily—and she was grateful that she wasn't alone.

"Unplanned, by Default, and in a Crisis"

Grandfamilies often form unexpectedly, sometimes instantly, and very few origin stories are positive. It may be because of the death of a parent, mental or physical illness, incarceration, opioid or other substance use, adverse immigration action, military deployment, or one of many other reasons. Substance abuse is an ever-increasingly common factor: A 2019 survey of grandfamilies showed that 40 percent of grandparent caregivers stepped in for this reason, compared to 21 percent in 2002. It's also one in which families are likely to be involved: Children who are removed from their homes because of parental drug or alcohol abuse are more likely to be placed with relatives than nonrelatives.[2]

In addition to the opioid crisis, other global health emergencies influence the numbers. This was evident most recently during the COVID-19 pandemic, which, in the United States, robbed more than 250,200 children of one or both of their caregivers.[3] Violence, particularly increasing gun violence, is another sadly common reason a grandfamily forms.

"There is always going to be some drug, some epidemic, some disaster, and grandfamilies should be the first line of defense for children," said child and family policy expert Mary Bissell. "That's never going to change, but what can change is the infrastructure to support them."

Adrian grew up in a multigenerational family, on the top floor of a two-family flat on Chicago's West Side that she shared with her parents and brother; her grandmother and uncle—and later her uncle's wife—lived downstairs. Babi, as her own Czech grandmother was known, was Adrian's after-school companion and protector against the boys who teased her for wearing the glasses she tried so hard to hide.

Adrian's father worked as a tool and die maker, and, as she remembers, they didn't have much. "Homegrown stuff," mostly, with a simple, useful philosophy: "Be there for everyone."

From the time Adrian was a child, one of her biggest goals was to have a close-knit family, surrounded by love. "I want all kids to have what I had," she said. "In school, when I got to sing solos, the whole first row and second row were my mom's family, my dad's family, and the neighbors. And I could always count with my Babi—she would put her finger in the air, counting the beats."

She wanted this most, of course, for her own children and grandchildren.

After a first marriage and divorce, Adrian married her husband Ron on her birthday; they were together for forty-one years. They each had two children, whom they included in a new, braided family. For their "funnymoon," they packed the four kids into Ron's Maverick and drove to Kings Island, a 364-acre amusement park and water park north of Cincinnati.

"We always had fun, me and Ron," said Adrian. He raised her two children like his own. "He never called himself [their] stepfather, and they never called him [their] stepfather," she says.

One of Adrian's two sons, Raymond, battled two demons, according to his doctor. He was bipolar and had "off the charts" Graves' disease, an autoimmune disorder that causes an overactive thyroid. Raymond told Adrian after his second attempt at suicide that he didn't like the way his body was functioning.

Because Raymond's on-and-off girlfriend, who became his wife, struggled with addiction, Joey was born addicted to cocaine and spent his first five days in the hospital. He was a very quiet baby, Adrian said. He barely moved, except when he had seizures. She stayed with him, rocking and singing to him. She was there so steadily that hospital staff often mistook her for his mother.

Eventually, the Illinois Department of Children and Family Services told Adrian and Ron that they had two choices—either take Joey, or he would be placed in foster care and become a ward of the state. There was only one answer: They fixed up a room in their house, which they'd bought for its proximity to senior centers, and prepared to bring Joey home.

"While the moment a grandfamily forms differs for everyone, there are some commonalities," said Dr. Joseph Crumbley, a nationally renowned kinship expert and a licensed clinical social worker with close to four decades of experience in private practice. He defines the formation of grandfamilies as "unplanned, by default, and in a crisis."[4]

Dr. Joseph Crumbley (2023). Photo credit: Kea Taylor.

There are many reasons for that immediate impulse to care for a young relative in need: loyalty, commitment, protection, care. "Grandparents sacrifice for their kids, and they sacrifice because it's love, you know," said Adrian.

Dr. Crumbley said that "[these] powerful motivating factors are reasons why in that instant, there is not even a question."

There is one more common theme, he added: "Shock and unpreparedness."

"You start thinking about finances," he continued. "You start thinking about housing, you start thinking about space. You start thinking about legal issues, custody issues for the children . . . food, clothing, education, medical issues . . ."

In a matter of moments, a relative caregiver is accountable not only for the child in need but also to the rest of their extended family. Identities shift abruptly with this new commitment. In some cases, family, friends, and colleagues are also absorbing the change.

The heads of grandfamilies usually find themselves at odds with something. Many come into the new relationship with already limited resources—a situation that will only be made tighter with more people at home.

Just as is true for the children in their care, the caregivers' well-being depends on the community that surrounds them. In both cases, with the right support, they can thrive.

When the relationship and the circumstances surrounding a grandfamily are strong, children's lives are changed. This is what author Michael Morris drove home to a crowd of grandfamilies gathered for a weekend of advocacy in Washington, DC.

"Every afternoon after lunch, my grandmother would have me sit in her lap and list out all of the people in my life who loved me," said Michael, whose novel *Slow Way Home* chronicles a story of a young man raised by his grandparents, based in part on his own experience.

"She passed away when I was nineteen, and not a day goes by that I don't think of her," Michael continued. "After all these years I can still see the expression in her eyes when she would tell me, 'You'll never know just how much I love you.' But now as an adult, I do know. She often told me that I was her investment, and I can only hope that she would be proud of the dividends that her time, teaching, and unconditional love have yielded."

New Routine, New Identity

When relative caregivers step into a parental role, it's a choice that often puts their own healthy habits and goals in the back seat. One study found that caregivers report being sleep-deprived, having poor eating and exercising habits, not taking time off when they are sick, and not making medical appointments for themselves.[5]

These challenges come at a time when their well-being is tied to a new generation. "I think traditionally people tend to think of their own health as being theirs, and when you're in a situation like we're in, you realize that your health is a big issue not just for you and not just for your spouse but for your grandchild as well," said grandfather Joe O'Leary in a StoryCorps interview.[6] "And so then, when COVID-19 comes along now, given our age and looking at the statistics of who is likely to be infected and suffer severe consequences from the infection, that raises the stakes of that game far, far higher and, of course, the stress that goes along with that."

Many relative caregivers new to raising children are also supporting other loved ones. For years, as Adrian cared for young Joey, she was also driving back and forth to check on her parents in the old neighborhood: "Little Village, where they were living, was changing, and we had a lot of gangs moving in," she said. After Adrian's father passed away, she brought her mother to come live with her, supporting her through a heart attack and later breast cancer.

At the same time, her son Raymond's disease was in full force. On April 29, 2009, he attempted suicide for a third time. This time he succeeded in taking his own life.

"He was a loving and caring person," Adrian said. "He would help around the house—cooking, gardening. Never had to tell him the floor needs to be washed." Recently, on what would have been Raymond's fifty-second birthday, Adrian wrote, "He came into our lives, curly blond hair, smile from ear to ear. He knew how to make us laugh and to cry . . . He gave us so much love . . . We love and miss him every day."

Like Adrian, many relative caregivers face life's most challenging circumstances as they try to chart a course for their new family. Caregivers of all ages may have experienced trauma. Grandparents and older relatives may have reached a point in their lives where they feel they know who they are and what they want. The dramatic shift required to step into a new role, often without warning, can impact their sense of identity—and their relationships.

One Kansas City grandmother had decided to redecorate, once her last child was grown and out of the house. She'd turned her condo into the dream home she'd always wanted—her version of Barbie's Dreamhouse. White carpets and crystal figurines decorated the living room. In her mind, it was a perfect place for a single woman. Then the knock came in the middle of the night. The authorities walked in with her two young grandchildren and left them.

The figurines were boxed up and put away in the closet.

The white carpet didn't stay white for long. Dreams deferred.

No longer will this grandmother play the role of special guest, a treasured second or third opinion, or a co-conspirator. No longer will the focus be on "spoiling" the grandchildren. Once people step into parental positions, they are the primary disciplinarians, providers, and protectors.

Dr. Crumbley says that this immediate change to preexisting relationships is a unique difference between grandfamilies and foster parents, who typically seek out and plan for a new addition to the family. "Before, you may have been an aunt, uncle, grandparent, mother, coach, teacher, godparent—all those previous roles and loyalties now get changed," he said. "In fact, they may even get reprioritized."

He calls the adjustment process for grandfamilies "three-dimensional," involving the child, their parent, and the relative caregiver. Depending on the circumstance, there are fourth and fifth dimensions too. "If you already have children at home," Dr. Crumbley says, "then they need to be prepared for the fact that other children are coming in—children who have been exposed to some kind of trauma."

In many cases, a new relative caregiver has a partner who must consider the child's potential role in their life. "You've got to get their consent and hope they buy into this decision that you've made out of commitment or loyalty," says Dr. Crumbley.

Mercedes Bristol was engaged to be married when she took in her infant grandson, followed quickly by her son's other four children. "[My fiancé] was a retired judge and very, very loving," said Mercedes, whose previous marriage had ended in divorce. "When we got [my grandson] Paul, [my fiancé] helped me with him," she said. "We started talking about getting married, looking at new homes. I was excited for that when we got the other four."

In addition to a new relationship with her grandchildren, the change created for Mercedes's fiancé the challenge of a different kind of relationship with her son. "He said, 'Your son is still wanting to be in the picture, and the kids cannot have two fathers,'" Mercedes said. He asked her to choose.

"My son kept telling me, 'Mom, I can co-parent with you,' and I believed him," Mercedes said. She broke off her engagement.

Ultimately, Mercedes spent thousands of dollars on legal bills to get her five grandchildren in her care, completed over sixty hours of training to become a licensed caregiver so she could get benefits for them, and retired early to take care of them and give them the loving home they deserved.

"Saying that I can't do this with another man because I don't want two different upbringings for the kids—that helped me," Mercedes said. "I've been single since 2009, and, you know, I'm happy. I didn't have anybody to argue with about what I was going to do with my grandchildren."

In many ways, a grandfamily's life depends on a caregiver's ability to manage stress and uncertainty, said Dr. Crumbley: "Recognizing what you're experiencing and making sure you get support for that becomes crucial in terms of helping the children manage the change."

Crucial indeed, and yet much easier said than done.

"Because my granddaughter was in so much pain after my daughter left her, all my focus was on helping her," said grandparent Jan Wagner. "I never had the chance to heal from my own loss, even though [my daughter] was still alive."[7]

Robyn Wind, Generations United's GRAND Voices support coordinator, maintained a close relationship with her son, Taylor, until he died. "Taylor's death has been the worst thing to happen to my family," she said. "He struggled but was well loved and respected not only by family but by our tribal community. I struggle daily . . . my longing for Taylor and the kisses he would plant on the top of my head is constant."

Each circumstance that creates a grandfamily impacts family members differently; grief and anger and relief are common and sometimes conflicting experiences.

After all, as Adrian reminds us, "Joey was born to two parents I loved."

Tenuous family relationships can complicate a relative caregiver's ability to set boundaries both personally and legally. Suing for legal custody or guardianship is a long, complicated process that is both financially and emotionally draining. To do so, a relative must prove that a child's parents are unfit. Parental rights and responsibilities must be severed, and the relative becomes the parent in the eyes of the law. These steps often rip families apart, rather than keeping them together.

Caregivers are often torn between helping their own son, daughter, or sibling while trying to prioritize the needs of the child in their care. "My son was in between homes, and I was trying to help him get on his feet," said Mercedes. "We were trying to get him to be responsible for his children."

Unfortunately, things didn't work out the way she hoped. "He would tell the kids he was coming and then didn't show up," she said. "I had to stop it. I had to say, 'You cannot do that. You're either in or out.'"

Relative caregivers may also feel a sense of regret. "I still get emotional about the connection with my son," said Victoria. "As a parent, I failed. In my mind, I failed. How did I let my son believe it was okay to live on the street and do drugs? From that, I was ashamed. I was depressed."

Psychologist Lenora Poe, in her groundbreaking book *Black Grandparents as Parents*, shared the words of one grandparent: "The awareness of our daughter's drug addiction was so painful and embarrassing to the whole family that we chose not to talk to anyone about what was going on in our family. We felt our family would be judged by our daughter's drug behavior. We felt alone, sad, and embarrassed because of what had happened to our family."[8]

Feelings of isolation are common among older relative caregivers. They're less likely to have friends going through similar experiences, which may have been the case when they were raising their own children. Their social circles change dramatically, as they are again handling car pools and bedtimes.

"I can't tell you how many friends I lost out on when they'd call on a Friday night, and I'd have to say, 'No, I can't go out with you; I got to get ready for soccer tomorrow,'" said grandmother Sarah Smalls. Indeed, people who step into the role of relative caregiver may not know where to turn for advice and support.

Strength in Numbers

The Brookdale Foundation's Relatives as Parents Program (RAPP) was way ahead of its time. It focused on support for caregivers outside the child welfare system—the majority of grandfamilies. It was established with a goal to assist local agencies in developing partnerships to meet the relative caregivers' various needs.

The number of support groups like Adrian's is growing, as more relatives raising children understand the benefits of building connections. These circles can provide comfort and inspire confidence, helping relative caregivers understand that they're not alone.

Support groups can also be valuable for grandfamilies

searching for help among an alphabet of agencies—most of which don't communicate with one another. When relative caregivers come together, they can find and share practical suggestions, resources, and other information that can be tough to come by.

"When I went to that first support group, I was in tears. You feel like you are the only one, and I sat in a room with five other grandparents who were going through the same thing as me—who actually gave me advice on a lot of things," said Victoria of her experience in the Duet Grandparents Raising Grandchildren support group in Phoenix, Arizona. "So, my going in my backyard and screaming all the time . . . that stopped. They literally saved me because I didn't know—we were drowning—I didn't know what to do, I didn't know where to go, I had nobody to call."

Researchers have proven the value of such connections. A recent study using the GrOW (Grandfamilies Outcome Workgroup) Support Group Scale found that 72 percent of participants felt better about being a caregiver when they attended a support group.[9]

Adrian called her first support group the Gift of Hope. The name echoed a conversation she'd had with another grandmother about what a gift their grandchildren were. "We are their hope," the grandmother said. Up to that point, Adrian said, the group had no name.

For the Gift of Hope, what began as small talk over coffee quickly developed into people helping people, and friendships grew deep. It was a place where caregivers could take a deep breath, moan if they felt like it, and receive the kind of encouragement from their peers, including Adrian, that they could carry forward in challenging moments.

New caregivers could express a need for household furnishings, and they would appear. An annual Christmas party became a lifeline for caregivers without gifts under the tree because they knew they'd leave with something for the kids. The meetings were so important, one grandmother took four buses to attend.

Adrian's message? "Don't be afraid. You have to have faith. The kids are what's important. Remember faith, not fear."

Or, as Dr. Crumbley often says, "You've got to be okay for the children to be okay."

Thankfully, the reverse is also true. Multigenerational living has been shown to improve the mental health of older adults.[10] Some grandparents say that they take better care of themselves because of the children, as they don't want to leave them alone. As one older caregiver said, "I can't die yet, I need to raise these kids."

"How Can I Figure This Out?"

GRAND Voice: Jan Wagner

I didn't wake up when I was fifty-seven years old and say, "Gosh, I want another baby." But my younger daughter had substance abuse issues. She came home expecting a baby; the guy had no desire to play a role. We tried to intervene in the substance abuse, and we brought her back home—to a house on our property.

I could tell right away that she wasn't connecting with the baby, Nessa. My older daughter, Stephanie, who worked for an infant and toddler early intervention program, said, "You know, there are a lot of developmental delays going on here, and I'm really concerned."

Finally, I started to say, "This kid is being neglected. I can't watch this happen." If someone would call me, worried, I'd say, "Don't call me, call protective services, please." Records were made, but nobody ever did anything.

Then, one day, my younger daughter said, "I'm going back to Grand Rapids."

"Well, I'll tell you what," I said. "Just leave me guardianship and leave the baby here."

She went to CPS (Child Protective Services), which told her that no one gives up guardianship voluntarily and that she should leave power of attorney. She scribbled that on a piece of paper. At her older sister's request, she also signed a paper that said that I could request evaluations for Nessa.

I came home from work one day and found a note that said she left. "Go pick up the baby at day care." And that was it.

We went through the evaluations with Nessa, and they confirmed that there was a lot of failure to thrive. She was two years old, nonverbal, not eating solid foods. She couldn't go up and down steps. She had never slept in a crib, and she didn't sleep at night. My husband and I now had this baby, and we were all just exhausted.

As far as CPS was concerned, this didn't point a finger to neglect. Still, my granddaughter was two, behaving as though she were, maybe, fifteen months. And that, as far as the evaluators were concerned, was a huge gap.

We had caseworkers begin immediately. They came out and taught us all sign language; they showed us how to work with Nessa's small motor skills and large motor skills.

All this time, I was just like a deer in the headlights.

As much as Nessa cried, she was also so distant. We didn't then realize that she didn't want to be touched. As she got older, we learned more and more. We had to ask to touch her: "Can I hug you? Can I give you a kiss?" A kiss on the top of her head—you could never do any more. Hug just a little.

She was just adorable, and the aunties wanted to pick her up. They'd approach her from behind, and she'd scream bloody murder.

One morning, about two years after Nessa began living with us, she was sitting in the family room with a cartoon on and she began to laugh. It struck me: I had never heard that sound before. What a bizarre thing!

I started looking into a support group for grandparents raising grandchildren, and I found there wasn't anything out there. I kept pounding on the doors of the Department of Health and Human Services (DHHS). I went directly to that CPS worker with frustration like you wouldn't believe. And what he told me was, "Well, if you insist that I open a case, I'm going to contact that mother. I'm going to tell her to come back and get her kid, and we'll keep an eye on it. But if she's living in Grand Rapids, you're not going to have any contact. If that child winds up in foster care and placed down in Grand Rapids or Kalamazoo or Chicago or wherever she happens to be, you're not going to know whether everything is okay or not. So long as the child is safe with you, you should go get guardianship from the court and leave it alone."

That made me run right straight to the court and file for guardianship. I was thinking that it would give some services. But what I realized was, poof! I screwed myself over.

I fell right into this caseworker's whole pattern—diversion. They had said, "Go get guardianship," because I already had the kid. They didn't have to support her. They didn't have to provide medical or any other kind of services to her or our family.

I went to all the training that DHHS and the national groups provided in my city, and that's how I learned what trauma was, and what adverse childhood experiences are, and failure to thrive. None of these things were part of my vocabulary; neither were "family court" or "social services." They just weren't: We were just your regular family with three kids, working our butts off to keep above water.

This is where my advocacy work began. I stood there and said to DHHS, and later to legislators, "How can you ignore this whole population? How can you not give these families this information? Why aren't you helping them?"

When you sit down with public officials, suddenly you get these theories: "This grandma never had any control over her own kids; what makes you think that she can do right this time?" The other big one was, "The apple doesn't fall too far from the tree." Honest to God, I even heard a legislator say that. What a joke.

We did and we continue to make accommodations for Nessa. We got her an IEP (Individualized Education Plan) and fought with the schools because they had no trauma training. We had her evaluated at multiple places—Easter-seals and DeVos Children's Hospital in Grand Rapids and many others.

Nessa had some health problems, including massive migraines that we thought were seizures. We tried different medications. The separation anxiety was a nightmare.

What I kept asking myself, over and over, was, How can I figure this out? *I had this kid, and I was going to save this kid's life, no matter what I did.*

I had been working all this time, but when my husband went on disability for cancer treatment, I stopped. We used our 401(k) to support Nessa, paying the penalty because we couldn't get services. When Ed lost his job and our insurance was canceled, we applied for benefits—Medicaid and food stamps and things like that. But first we had to spend down our 401(k). This is why most grandparents raising grandchildren also don't have any retirement funds.

We've always been outside the system. This is how it goes without having the support systems intact and having to fight all this way yourself. I've had to teach myself, learn myself, beg, steal, and borrow, to try and find what is offered.

As much as I disagreed with the legislators' stereotypes, deep down, I wanted every bit of my own circumstance to be my fault. I had raised Nessa's mother; somehow, I was responsible. My other two kids would say, "But you have us, and we're successful. And we have college degrees, and we have kids and homes."

They said, "It just happens." But I had long thought that if I were responsible for my daughter's behavior, I could fix it.

I'd tried everything: Manipulate, lose my cool, send voicemails and messages and whatever else, but I never fixed her. When we got Nessa, my first focus was to fix her situation, but through my own understanding of trauma and mental health, I learned that I couldn't do that: I couldn't fix the trauma, but I could certainly help her through it.

This—letting go of taking personal responsibility for everyone—was my aha moment. Now, I try to focus on the fact that I'm a lot stronger than I thought I was. I'm a lot more capable. I'm a lot less fearful. I can take a challenge and hit it head-on. That's how I take care of myself.

CHAPTER THREE:

Suitcases Come in All Sizes: Trauma

> "I thought because my grandkids were babies (six months, one and a half, and two and a half), they were not going to have any problems. Boy, was I wrong! They had problems with separation anxiety; it was so painful to see them go through this. I had to tell them a hundred times a day how much I loved them and was never going to leave them."
>
> —Delia Martinez, grandmother, San Antonio, Texas[1]

When Bob Ruble's niece came to live with him, she was eight years old and had, sadly, experienced years of abuse and neglect. He felt challenged by some of her behaviors. He wasn't always sure how best to respond.

"I didn't know how to deal with trauma, so when [my niece] engaged me, I would engage her back," he said. "And then I learned that that's not the right thing to do.

"She'd push my buttons, doing this or that, and then I would walk away," he continued. "She'd say, 'Yeah, there you go, just like everybody else in my life, walking away from me.' I didn't know how to deal with that."

He needed help, he said: "I started learning more. I actually had to look [up] things like, 'What is trauma?'"

If, as Dr. Crumbley said, so many grandfamilies' stories are rooted in trauma, then it's little wonder the road they travel can feel rough and uncertain. A serious break in the connection between parent and child, no matter the reason, can impact that child profoundly—both in the moment and for years and decades to come.

"I didn't understand that my niece walked into this house with this big, invisible suitcase full of crap that I had no knowledge or understanding of," said Bob. "By high school especially, there are a lot of [bad] influences there. You try to do everything that you can so that you get to the other side, and everybody survives."

Navigating unknown territory and trying to unpack a childhood of painful memories is part of many grandfamilies' stories. "For the caregiver, [there's] the shock of unpreparedness, the ambivalence, the anxiety . . . you're definitely moving down the curve of a traumatic experience," said Dr. Crumbley.

For children, he said, "the mere fact of that emotional separation is traumatic."

He says that a grandfamily's family ties are a huge advantage over foster care placement. Relatives can share a sense of loss and feelings of abandonment.

"It's easier in a family crisis and less traumatic for the kids to go with someone they know and love," said Larry Cooper, executive vice president of innovation for Florida's Children's Home Network, which has been working with kinship families since 2001.

While the word "trauma" can be overused, it does have an official definition. The National Substance Abuse and Mental Health Services Administration defines it as an event, series of events, or set of circumstances that is experienced by an individual as physically or psychologically harmful or life-threatening and that has lasting adverse effects on the individual's functioning and mental, physical, social, emotional, or spiritual well-being.[2]

Children who enter the child welfare system are far more likely to have been exposed to traumatic events known as adverse childhood experiences (ACEs). These include substance abuse; physical, emotional, or sexual abuse; and chronic neglect. About one out of every four children living in grandfamilies were neglected before coming into their relatives' care. A similar number lived with their parents' substance abuse.[3]

These children have a much higher likelihood of experiencing similar challenges than their peers.[4] As was once the case for Bob's niece, they can also have a tough time developing and maintaining healthy relationships.

Families from cultures that have been systematically oppressed also have to manage trauma that has been passed down through generations of survivors.

Richard Henry Pratt, the founder of the first off-reservation boarding school for Native American children, is infamously credited with the phrase "Kill the Indian, save the man." This belief in assimilating Indigenous populations for their own good guided his work at the Carlisle Indian Industrial School.[5] At the time, forcible removal of children from their families was considered a progressive idea. Now we know it was a form of cultural genocide, severing language and traditions.

"I remember being at [my grandparents'] home, and if someone came to the door, we were told to hide," said Robyn Wind during a 2020 episode of the *Generations United* podcast. "My spot was behind the couch."[6]

GRAND Voice Robyn Wind (2025). Photo credit: Generations United.

Robyn holds tribal citizenship with the Muscogee (Creek) Nation. American Indian and Alaska Natives (AI/AN) endured more than two hundred years of policies intended to exterminate, remove, or assimilate them. Her own father was raised by his grandparents, who, she says, were "products of Indian boarding schools.

"I didn't understand why [we hid]," she continued. She also had the same reaction to the doorbell and ran behind the couch when she was with her maternal grandparents, who are not Indian. "They'd laugh and say, 'Oh she's just shy,'" Robyn said.

"Now that I'm older, I know they were taken to boarding school and people were just rounded up and just taken off," she said. "I understand that."

Robyn has worked in Indian Child Welfare for fifteen

years. Her son Taylor struggled, and on May 19, 2014, she got her three-month-old grandson, Jack, whom she's been raising for eleven years.

"When my kids were younger, when people knocked on the door, I'd say, 'Shush, go to your room.' I had to learn and understand why we did that. There are so many factors, due to historical trauma that we've been through."

Grandfamilies cope as best they can with these profound challenges. For Jan Wagner, her granddaughter's pain was so deep it felt almost impossible to overcome. "No matter what, I think she will forever remember running down the driveway chasing after her mother," she said. "It's just there. It's in her body."

For families like this, help is essential. Stress might be managed, but trauma needs specialized support.

Grandfamilies Tend to Wounds Others Can't See

Adam Otto was nine years old when his paternal grandparents, Annie and Jack Otto, got custody of him; he moved in with them in Hedgesville, West Virginia. His mom struggled with bipolar disorder and frequently lost custody of him; his father, who had custody, died of heart disease but not before he signed paperwork granting Annie and Jack custody of Adam. The trauma that Adam experienced in his early life, including his mother kidnapping him when he was in the third grade, had a lasting effect on his behavior and his sense of safety.

Diagnosed with ADHD, Adam often acted out in school. Annie believed that some of the people at the child welfare agency didn't fully acknowledge the extent of Adam's need.

"Behavioral problems are a sign of something else," she said. "If something goes wrong, the first question should be what happened to that child last night? Why is he acting that way, and what can I do to make it better?"

Adam also had trouble sleeping and was often afraid that he might be taken away from his grandparents. Given the changes and uncertainty he had experienced, he had severe separation anxiety from his grandmother, especially when she had to travel for her growing advocacy efforts as part of the Generations United GRAND Voices Network. Even when he was a teenager, he found leaving home to go to summer camp particularly difficult.

Annie and Jack supported Adam through his challenges the best way they knew how: by reassuring him that they would always love and care for him, reading to him every night before bed and staying with him until he fell asleep, and making sure he had counselors he could talk to about his feelings.

The first year Adam lived with them, Jack got up early every day to drive him to the school he had been attending so he could stay with his favorite teacher. He continued with this daily ritual well into high school, in part because it was less time than the school bus, but also it protected him from being bullied on the ride home. When Adam started college, leaving his grandparents was tough, so his grandfather drove him to school and brought him home on weekends.

"I was lucky because my grandparents acknowledged [that] I needed help they couldn't provide and were financially stable and able to afford mental health and other supports for me," said Adam. "But more needs to be done to ensure that all children have access to good mental health services and [that] the professionals who work with them really understand how trauma affects children and their families."

Annie said that the first line of defense against trauma is the love and unconditional support of family, but the government and broader community also have a responsibility to be "the safety net for the safety net." They must make sure that caregivers have the financial and other services they need to help children overcome challenges, tap into their own resilience, and build a stable and happy future.

After graduating from college, Adam worked for a few years and decided he wanted to be a lawyer. He took the Law School Admission Test (LSAT) and was accepted into American University's law school, where he graduated second in his class. He started full-time at a law firm after graduating; he requested, and the firm agreed, that his pro bono portfolio includes grandfamilies. "Adam is his own greatest success story," said a proud Annie. "I tell people he is living proof that children can overcome hardship."

"My grandparents always let me know that they love me no matter what happens or what I do," says Adam. "Their love and consistent reassurance that they were there for me really made a big difference for me."

Jack, Adam, and Annie Otto (2018). Photo credit: Generations United.

Chad Dingle had come to live with his grandmother, Joan, after his mother, Joan's daughter, was arrested. Chad's mother and her two male roommates spanked him, off and on, for more than four hours when he wouldn't eat. He was diagnosed with PTSD at age four.

"When I used to get so angry, it was like I was drunk and didn't know what was going on," Chad said. "Later I'd think, *What just happened?* I didn't know how I had gotten to the point of being out of control."

It took Joan a while to get custody of him. She was first suspected by state workers of being a "bad" parent because of the behavior of her daughter (who got into drugs and alcohol). Joan was able to finally convince the state that Chad was her first priority, and she became a foster parent. This meant she received a small check to help meet his needs and, most important, find counseling for Chad.

"One counselor who he liked and trusted turned him around," Joan said. "She told him, 'Life is a puzzle, and the pieces we each pick or reject form us.' She helped him identify what was good and bad in his birth parents and what he wanted for himself."

Joan went on to write *Second Time Around: Help for Grandparents Who Raise Their Children's Kids*. "I learned a lot of things I wished I didn't know. I didn't know that traumatized kids' brains are permanently altered," said Joan. "If I had realized that, unlike most of us, his emotions started at alert or alarm instead of calm, I would have tweaked some of my parenting approaches."

The reality is that most kinship families will need help at some point, Joan explained. Most only need a little more help when things first go wrong and then just a boost if something pops up later, but the needs and timing are different for every family, she added. Sometimes, it's something as simple as a babysitter for two hours; other times, it's more complex.

Challenges with Health Care Access

Federal and state health insurance coverage programs like Medicaid or the Children's Health Insurance Program are crucial for families like the Dingles. Joan's granddaughter also came to live with her briefly, when her daughter was homeless.

"I had a note from my daughter giving me 'custody' and a state medical card," Joan said. "The state-provided medical insurance was a great help, as she had not been to a dentist in five years and had gum and teeth problems. We were able to get her new glasses, and medical attention for a vaginal infection that she said she'd had for a month."

Unfortunately, these programs can only help when a caregiver knows how to pursue them.

A grandmother who worked at Vanderbilt University said that when she got custody of her grandson, he'd been living on the streets with her son, the child's father. His dental care was nonexistent, and he arrived with a mouthful of problems. It wasn't until she spent down her retirement savings to have his teeth fixed that she learned she could have accessed the Tennessee Children's Health Insurance Program, TennCare Kids, which would have covered it all. Too late for her, but not too late for her to educate new caregivers who came to the Nashville support group she attended.

Adrian had a similar story. When she began caring for Joey, she didn't know about the Illinois All Kids health care plan. She and Ron began paying out of pocket for Joey's substantial medical needs, which often required three or four doctor appointments a week. It wasn't until she was driving one day and saw a billboard advertising the program that she learned his health care could have been paid for by the state. She immediately enrolled Joey in the program that no one had told her existed.

As one grandmother told her fellow support group members at a meeting in Los Angeles: "When I meet with an intake worker, I never take no for an answer. I keep asking, and asking, and asking. Persistence can pay off when information isn't readily available. It is frustrating when you have to wait all day, miss work, and then let them [the workers] be rude to you."

Support is out there, for both short- and long-term medical needs. This includes funding in some states to help families who have children with disabilities. "Family support" funds may pay for equipment like a ramp into the house or a van lift.

Families just need to know about it.

Children's health care advocacy is personal for Wisconsin Senator Tammy Baldwin, who was raised by her maternal grandparents, David and Doris Green. Her grandfather, a biochemist, was a professor at the University of Wisconsin–Madison. Her grandmother became chief costumer in the university's theater department. "My grandparents were empty nesters," she reflected during an interview. "They probably were thinking about a life of retirement, and then they get this little infant they raise until I go off to college."[7]

In 2017, while accepting a lifetime achievement award from Generations United, Senator Baldwin shared the difficulties her grandparents faced when she was nine and spent three months in the hospital with an illness similar to spinal meningitis. That was when her grandparents learned that their health insurance didn't cover grandchildren. Because she was then considered to be a child with a preexisting

Tammy Baldwin with her grandparents. Courtesy of Tammy Baldwin.

condition, they couldn't find any insurance company to cover her when she was growing up.

This experience led her to believe the system was broken. Access to high-quality, affordable health care became the issue that brought her to public life.

Because of her grandfamily's experience, Senator Baldwin wrote the Affordable Care Act amendment that allows young people to stay on their parents' health insurance until age twenty-six.

"Tonight I want to talk about family," said Senator Baldwin when speaking at the 2024 Democratic National Convention. "We know all families don't look alike. My mother was a teenager when I was born. She struggled with addiction. I never met my father. But I had two incredible grandparents who stepped in and raised me. Everything I know, I learned from them. In every way a child needs, my grandparents were there for me. As they grew older, it was my privilege to be there for them." A grand success paying tribute to the grandparents she loved.[8]

A Chance to Rest

Grandfamilies need resources and services, but they also need acknowledgment, understanding, and respect for the choices and sacrifices they've made. This is especially true for caregivers supporting children who are living with illness, a disability, or other special needs.

"Respite" is a concept—a pause, a refuge. The ARCH National Respite Network and Resource Center, for example, defines it as "planned or emergency care provided to a child or adult with special needs in order to provide temporary relief to family caregivers."[9] The specifics can vary greatly, as do a caregiver's needs.

Respite comes in different forms.

One day, a Family Friends Program respite worker arrived at a grandmother's house, where she was pointed to the children's room. She walked in, assuming their caregiver would go shopping or get her hair done. After greeting the children, the respite worker walked back out only to find the grandmother lying on the floor. When she told the older woman she should go do something for herself, the grandmother replied, "I just want to lay here." Clearly, she was exhausted.

Respite programs can serve the entire family. In 2017, San Diego County demonstrated this when staff launched an innovative program for grandfamilies: Gramping—a free, overnight camping experience.

"We learned through surveys that kinship families were eager for more activities that strengthen family bonds, especially since many of the children have been through trauma and disruption in their lives," said Pam Plimpton, intergenerational coordinator for the County of San Diego Health and Human Services Agency.

Co-created with the Department of Parks and Recreation, the first Gramping event was held at Dos Picos County Campground in Ramona, California. Camping equipment was provided for the eighteen kinship caregivers and thirty children who needed it because some had never been camping before. It was a bonus that they didn't have to travel far from their homes to find themselves looking at rolling hills and open fields surrounded by people to care for them. At this site, a large central grassy area was perfect for pitching all the tents, so the kids could play together when they weren't in planned activities.

Over the course of two days, county staff lead activities like games and crafts, "gentle" hikes, tree planting, roasting marshmallows around the campfire to make s'mores, and a glow-stick dance-off. They treat the grands to supper and breakfast the following day, which prompted one caregiver to say, "As a senior raising a special needs child, it was wonderful to have an event where I didn't have to do all the work!"

"By immersing participants in a nature-based, stress-free setting, Gramping allows caregivers and children to reset, recharge, and reconnect," said Pam. "Nature is healing. It's a fun way to promote intergenerational bonding, caregiver resilience, child development—all leading to healthier and more stable families." She followed up, smiling, "Being part of this event has truly been a highlight of my career."

It works. Feedback has been overwhelmingly positive. One grandparent said that Gramping "brought us closer by doing an all-family activity, sleeping in the same tent, and having no distractions." Another echoed this sentiment when she noted the value of experiencing "quality time with no electronics."

Since then, the county has sponsored five Gramping events, and the event has been growing in size over the years. Wait lists are now the norm.

GrandRallies, GRAND Voices Network, Grand Results—a Family Affair

Resources like respite care, while still tough to come by, are much easier to find than they were thirty years ago. That's thanks in large part to advocates like attorney and child and family policy expert Mary Bissell.

In 1999, Mary was working on the staff of the Children's Defense Fund (CDF). This leading advocacy and research organization was founded by Marian Wright Edelman, a civil rights and children's rights advocate who worked closely with Dr. Martin Luther King Jr. during the Civil Rights Movement. Mary was mentored by the legendary MaryLee Allen, who coauthored CDF's first policy report with Hillary Rodham, now Hillary Clinton—the only other staff member at the time.

MaryLee was a giant in the child welfare field, respected for her compassion, deep knowledge, and brilliance as a strategist. She knew that Mary had a deep commitment to kinship families, developed when she did pro bono work while a law student at Georgetown University. Her passion deepened as a fellow in Senator Jay Rockefeller's office working closely with Barbara Pryor. Together they skillfully cultivated bipartisan support for key kinship legislation. MaryLee encouraged her mentee to pursue her passion: connecting advocates and grassroots leaders to change policy in support of grandfamilies. She understood that the families formed whenever there was a need—whether it was Black migration, a substance abuse crisis, or an economic downturn.

"It's clear kin should be the first perfect cover for children," Mary said. "It's never going to change; there's always something, so we need to change the infrastructure to support them."

Mary pulled together groups like Generations United, AARP, and the Brookdale Foundation to create GrandFacts, fact sheets for every state, and identify grassroots leaders. This led to a gathering at CDF's Alex Haley Farm, a 157-acre retreat center designed for building movements and encouraging spiritual renewal.

Alex Haley, author of *The Autobiography of Malcolm X* and *Roots*, among other books, loved East Tennessee, where he had lived with his grandparents for the first years of his life and then in the summers. He bought the farm outside of Clinton, Tennessee, planted 220 apple trees that produced fruit to be cooked up for the many guests he entertained, and invited his neighbors once a year to harvest. Marian Wright Edelman, looking for a retreat center, found the farm after Haley died and turned it into the perfect spot for training and reflection.

Mary remembers the retreat as being a joyful gathering of grassroots advocates from thirty-nine states who lived, ate, and prayed side by side with national advocates. Their time together proved essential to the national advocacy effort, helping to tighten bonds between state leaders and their national allies.

In 2003, this group collaborated to organize the first GrandRally, a gathering of grassroots advocates to raise awareness of grandfamilies on Capitol Hill and beyond.

Adrian took home a flyer for the event from her very first support group meeting; it's the only thing she remembers getting out of it. After reading it carefully, she called her son Tim—at midnight. A twenty-four-year military veteran, Tim, along with his wife and two children, lived and worked in the DC area. He said he was going to send her the ticket and go with her.

He did.

In October 2003, as Adrian and Tim walked through the mass of grandparents and relative caregivers gathering on the grounds of the US Capitol, where the rally was being staged, they both started to cry. Adrian hadn't seen Tim cry since he fell off his bike when he was a little kid.

"Mom," Tim said, "this is where you'll find your answers."

The first GrandRally brought together 850 caregivers and their supporters, representing twenty-eight states. At the time, grandparents, other relatives, and close family friends were raising close to 2.8 million children outside of the formal foster care system. They were saving our nation an average of $6.5 billion per year.[10]

Adrian balked—more than $6 billion! It was a cruel irony: Relative caregivers, an essential support system for their own family, are also a social safety net. Despite all the myths and dismissive stereotypes, grandfamilies were not asking for a handout. While they stretch their limited incomes, they are creating huge savings for taxpayers.

Seeing so many people in a similar circumstance, advocating for change, Adrian understood just how much grandfamilies were providing a service to the country and should be respected. She went back to Illinois determined to become an advocate in her home state.

Adrian's response was just what Mary had hoped for, back when her fingers were turning purple from tying helium balloons for the rally. That day, she juggled a phone call from Senator Ted Kennedy's office and a question from port-a-potty vendor Royal Flush about where to go. MaryLee told Mary not to worry about her fingers; they'd recover. When they stood together as the music signaled the beginning of the rally, watching the grands sway and hug, she knew MaryLee was right.

MaryLee Allen and Mary Bissell at the 2003 GrandRally.
Photo credit: Children's Defense Fund.

Advocacy groups have long organized "Hill Days," when their members rally from around the country and plan visits with their members of Congress. It's rare to be in Washington, DC, on a day without groups of people proudly wearing name tags and often matching colors, carrying folders full of issue briefs and talking points, heading with purpose to Senate and House office buildings. For some it's their first time; others are experienced and may even know shortcuts to get to the next office on their itinerary. Comfortable shoes are also a sign that it's not their first rodeo. It helps to have a specific policy ask—and even better if it's related to legislation that has been or is about to be introduced.

Why do organizations like Generations United and countless other interest groups keep putting the time and money into coordinating and preparing constituents? Because when done well, constituent meetings can be incredibly impactful and lead to results a paid lobbyist could only dream of achieving.

Adrian spoke at the second GrandRally in 2005 and made it a priority to be at every rally after that. She remembers meeting with her representatives, including Congressman Danny Davis, who taught at the high school she attended, and Senator Dick Durbin. She smiles when she thinks about meeting with a freshman senator named Barack Obama.

She had her mother, Double Babi, with her, and Senator Obama kept referring to her as "Toot," because she reminded him of the grandmother who raised him. When they were getting ready to leave, he hugged her, saying, "I just need to hug you for what you're doing. We need people to protect our children. We need people who care about other people in this boat."

The 2008 GrandRally was emceed by communications executive Stacey Walker, who, with his sister, was raised by

Left to right: Sen. Barack Obama, Adrian's mom, Adrian Charniak, Sen. Dick Durbin (2005). Courtesy of Adrian Charniak.

his grandmother in Cedar Rapids, Iowa, after the murder of their mother, when Stacey was just four years old.

The grandfamilies loved him. He was confident, inspiring, and engaging, giving the grands hope because of the grand success he'd become. After the rally, he went on a Hill visit to meet with a staff member for Iowa Senator Charles Grassley to talk about the need for supportive policies for grandfamilies. He launched into his pitch. When he stopped, the staffer said, "You had me at hello." Senator Grassley signed onto the Fostering Connections to Success and Increasing Adoptions Act and became an important champion who helped it become law later that year.

JJ Hitch was just twenty-one when he spoke at the rally and shared a poem of hope he'd written for children being raised in grandfamilies. The rally also featured the

Stacey Walker emceeing the 2008 GrandRally. Photo Credit: William Libro.

Second Chance Choir, from the pioneering Pittsburgh-based, kinship-serving A Second Chance, Inc., founded by renowned expert Dr. Sharon McDaniel. The choir delivered a moving rendition of Bill Withers's tribute to his own grandmother, "Grandma's Hands." Elvis impersonator Tim Dudley, who was raised by his grandparents, charmed the grands, singing and passing out signature Elvis scarves. He dedicated his performance to his grandmother, who worked a part-time job to fund his trip to Washington, DC.

Tim credits his grandmother for encouraging him to pursue his dreams. He became an Elvis fan when he was just three years old. Back then, Tim asked his grandmother to pin a towel on his shirt to mimic Elvis's cape, and after just one day of that improvised costume (plus the fact that he ripped holes in his T-shirts), his grandmother decided to make him his first Elvis suit.

Around the same time, many states began establishing and running kinship navigator programs. Like GrandFacts, these programs are central places for grandfamilies to go for helpful information. In 2008 and again in 2012, there was a competitive grant program, Family Connection Grants, to support these efforts. In 2018, Congress voted to set aside funding that states could compete for and match to start the programs.

States participating in kinship navigator programs have found them to be a cost-effective, efficient method of service delivery. Unfortunately, there isn't always a "there there" to which families can navigate. The demand for services simply exceeds the resources or funding available. Still, the programs have proven to be, and continue to be, resources—especially for families just stepping into the caregiving role, who often don't know where to turn for help.

For more than a quarter century, through Capitol Hill visits, Senate hearings, rallies, op-eds, and more, grandfamilies have shined a light on their families' crucial role in American life. Given their depth of experience and unwavering commitment to the children in their care, who better to educate members of Congress and their staff about the invaluable role they play in raising our country's children?

That's why, in 2014, with support from Casey Family Programs, Generations United created the GRAND Voices Network, a national advocacy group comprising caregiver advocates, including grandparents, aunts, uncles, cousins, siblings, other relatives, and close family friends raising children whose parents cannot.

The GRANDs, as we call them, bring their real-life stories to media interviews, hearings on Capitol Hill, convenings at the White House, and legislative events in their home states; they also provide input on proposed legislation, draft publications, and essential data collection tools. Their "lived experience" makes abstract ideas real and numbers less anonymous.

"Being part of GRAND Voices is like having a PhD," said Adrian, who became one of the first GRANDs in 2014. "People like titles," she continued. "It tells them I do know something, and they listen." She went on to say of the bond between GRANDs, "It connects you and lets the love that you have for your family travel to another family. It's a group of caring people helping each other."

We began with representatives from five states; by 2025 we had GRANDs in more than forty-six states and thirteen tribes. Throughout this time, they have demonstrated the power and impact of meaningful engagement, changing public policy and service delivery systems across the country.

"You did 'lived experience' before it was a thing. And you did it better than anyone else," said Sarah Gesiriech, a former staffer in the office of Iowa Senator Charles Grassley, who introduced key legislation in support of grandfamilies.

"You made it practical—like, grandparents can't get their kids enrolled in school," she said. "You made me understand it could be any family, any time, and you painted a legitimate picture of the families. Your staff could articulate the case for the families and meet with anyone on either side of the aisle."

We continue to uplift grandfamilies' personal experiences because we know how much they impact leaders and lawmakers across the political spectrum. Still, for our movement, like so many others, forward progress is neither predictable nor easy.

As a leading national advocate for children and families, MaryLee Allen often referred to the "cicada rule" of child welfare policy change. Just like the appearance of buzzing cicadas, meaningful federal child welfare legislation always seemed to happen in seven-year cycles.

Sen. Chuck Grassley and former foster youth being raised by sister (2014).
Photo credit: Generations United.

MaryLee believed that advocates and grandfamilies needed to be ready for these opportunities—and that sharing their stories with policymakers at events like the GrandRally was the very best preparation.

"Don't Be a Victim."

GRAND Voice: Mercedes Bristol

My son had four children with his second wife. They had challenges, and CPS got involved. In 2010, there was another CPS case, and I had the kids for about four months. Then all four were returned to their mother, who was, by then, my son's ex-wife.

Then my son had another baby with his girlfriend. Paul was born in December 2010 with acute breathing problems—a lot of health issues. CPS was also involved there, so Paul came to live with me in March 2011. By the end of the year, the other four kids were removed for the third time and also placed with me.

At that point I went back to the attorney who had helped me get custody papers for Paul. "We need to do an intervention," I said. "We cannot have these kids going back and forth. Every removal is another trauma." So, she represented me, and we did this intervention.

It was really hard. The mom [of the four kids] would go to the school sometimes; one time she smelled like liquor. The school knew of my situation and was protective of the children. At that time, when I got there, some of the kids were inside the office, waiting. She was still there, causing a scene with one of the children as the principal was trying to get her off the school premises.

I tried to help my son get on his feet. "You can stay here," I told him. "Start working and get yourself responsible. Get an apartment so you can save money."

He would tell the kids he was coming and not show up. "You cannot do that," I had to tell him. "You're either in or out. You cannot promise the kids something and not do it."

It went on for a year—a hard year, but working with that, I ended up adopting five kids.

I was really depressed. I was fifty-seven years old, recently single, working for the state as a social worker, working for my retirement. At the time, the two youngest weren't in school; three of the kids were in three different day cares. Four out of the five children had ADHD, and two had oppositional defiant disorder. I got them medical help, but I still had to manage it all.

I got two car seats, and the two middle ones squeezed in the back with them; the nine-year-old would sit in the front with me because she was a bigger girl. I'd applied for one-time TANF (Temporary Assistance for Needy Families) but was denied because our car was over the resource limit. A six-year-old car that was paid off, that I'd bought with the divorce settlement I got from my ex-husband. It almost works against you if you have anything.

I was thinking I was a victim: I didn't ask for these kids. At one point, I even cried to the Lord, and I said, "I can't do this, Lord." We were in church, and with all these bodies next to me, I thought, They need a mother and a father. They don't need a grandmother. I can't do this.

I really heard Him saying to stop being a victim and be proactive—that these were His children, and He would take care of them and take care of me. So, I said, "Okay, I'm gonna trust you." And that's what we did.

The attorney was able to do the adoption for the kids. Once I adopted through the state, they gave me $400 for each child.

My doctor was very, very wise. He gave me medication and then he sent me to Al-Anon, where I learned that it wasn't my fault. I didn't cause it; I can't cure it. I could only empower myself.

I was still working, paying for the day care and somebody to pick up the kids after school. I got home at six and then rushed to do dinner if I hadn't made it the night before. Then I had to get the three kids' homework done and get them to bed by eight. Later, I got the three older kids into a learning center, so they would help them with homework. I had to pay for that too.

In 2016, I did my budget. After all that, I was only going to have $300 left in my purse for working full-time. I thought, well, if I apply for food stamps, I will make ends meet and be able to be home, raising the kids. I'm grateful that I was able to think about that. That's how I supported the kids.

Every morning, after taking the kids to day care and to school, I would stop at church to hear mass. I would talk to these ladies, and they all said they prayed for me.

"I need help," I would tell them. "Do you know any babysitter, somebody, you know, a nanny or somebody?" And all they would say is, "We're going to pray. We're going to pray for you." I got resentful; I needed hands.

One night Paul's fever spiked to 105 in the middle of the night. I thought, What do I do? *I didn't have anybody to watch the four kids in the middle of the night! I put them in the car, and I took them to the fire department, which was very close.*

As soon as I got there, they packed him with ice, and they took him in the ambulance. There I go with my other four kids behind the ambulance. We were at the hospital all night with all five kids . . . Those were hard times.

God provided everything. I was able to hire a girl who would come in three times a week at four o'clock in the afternoon on Mondays, Wednesdays, and Thursdays, to cook for us and clean for me. Some days she came from four to eight, and when dinner was done, she would help me give the kids a bath and put them to bed. Then I was able to function. It helped a lot.

One night, while I was watching TV with my aunt, there was a program called Dancing with the Children. "That might help the kids, if you put them in this program," she said. The program was too far away, but they had a support group called Abuelos y Nietos Juntos—Grandparents and Grandchildren. I started going to that. It was led by Dr. Santos, who had done research about how many Hispanic grandparents were raising grandchildren. She became my mentor.

"There have to be other grandparents out there," I told Dr. Santos. "How could we reach other grandparents?" She connected me with Generations United.

"Can we do more support groups?" I asked.

"No," she said, "but I'll help you."

I went to my kids' school, where I had been very well supported, and started with a flyer and an event—a cafecito, or coffee, with the principal. There, I did my little spiel about a support group. We had one grandmother who was raising her grandkids who got so involved that we started putting dates together and going around to all the schools with flyers. Now we have twenty-six support groups across the state.

It's incredible. God told me, "Don't be a victim; be proactive." I didn't know what He meant at the time, but we raised awareness. I started talking to legislators here in San Antonio.

"Go talk to Senator Menendez," I told the grandparents, and they did. He saw that we were serious. Now, he comes to our events. He does a lot of work with us. Right now, we've served two thousand grandparents and then some.

My story is a whole lot of people's stories—I know, having spoken with so many grandfamilies throughout the years. I work to raise awareness of the lack of support and resources across the board. It's so hard, as so many of the challenges are related and connected. When you talk about financial need, it's so related to education, to health care.

The bottom line is that we have to build community one city at a time. We are now in Houston, in Dallas, and in Fort Worth. People across Texas send me messages: "Do you have that program here?"

"No," I say, "but if you want to be the voice, I can train you right; I can make sure that you have the right message and you're reaching other grandparents."

That's why we're applying for grants. We're praying that we can train a lot of other voices like mine and get them to be proactive too.

CHAPTER FOUR:

All Politics Is Local: Education Challenges

"I realized this was the first year my grandchild has started and finished the year at the same school . . . and she's in the sixth grade."

—Grandmother during a support group meeting at Los Angeles's Jewish Family Services, 2003

Jackie Chong was a grassroots rabble-rouser—more a ringleader than a stay-at-home grandmother. The short, round, native Hawaiian grandmother of Tahitian-Japanese-French ancestry loved to laugh as she wheeled around Honolulu in her oversized sedan. She would give rides to other grandmothers and conspire with them on how to change Hawaiian laws that interfered with relatives living their cultural value of *ohana* (family, kinship), which extends across generations caring for each other.

The grandmothers who were snug in her back seat were members of the Na Tutu (Hawaiian for "all"—*na*—and "grandmother"—*tutu*) Grandparents Raising Grandchildren, a small, passionate committee of advocates formed by the Windward Oahu Family and Community Education Council. Their mission: seek necessary legislation that would allow relatives to raise children in safe, loving, and secure homes. They were determined to not just rock babies; they were going to rock the boat and change laws.

At the top of their list were consent laws—laws that enable relatives to make decisions for children without the involvement of their parents.

Back then, and still in many places today, extended family caring for children without a legal connection couldn't enroll children in school, let alone access the special education services many of them needed. These caregivers couldn't take part in school activities designed to involve parents. (Consent to obtain medical care was a closely connected issue.)

The barriers contradicted what Jackie knew, from experience, to be in the children's best interests. Her home and surrounding grounds, overlooking the Koolau mountains on the windward side of Oahu, were filled with the laughter of her children and grandchildren. This included daughter Donna and Donna's son Kale, who lived with Jackie and knew her as Bamma—as did Jackie's husband.

Jackie was born in Hilo on Mother's Day 1933, a fitting day for someone who centered her life and work on ohana. Her work with the Na Tutu was not her first experience with grassroots advocacy: In 1978, she was elected to serve as a Con Con delegate to the Hawaii State Constitutional Convention, a watershed event designed to help right the wrongs done toward native Hawaiians since the overthrow of the Kingdom of Hawai'i in 1893.

Jackie's daughter Donna was just one of the family members and friends she asked to join her in campaigning by holding up signs along a busy roadway.

Like many other relative caregivers, Jackie was resourceful and relentless when it came to advocating for the children in her care. On behalf of the Na Tutu, she contacted Ana Beltran, who is now Generations United's director of the Grandfamilies & Kinship Support Network. Jackie knew about Ana, who is a lawyer by training and a committed grandfamilies advocate, because she was a speaker on a 2001 national video teleconference on kinship care issues that inspired the formation of the Na Tutu. Ana tracked state legislation relevant to kinship families. She helped guide Jackie to California's education consent law, which the Na Tutu determined best fit Hawaii's legislative interests.

California started the education consent wave in 1994, close to a decade before the Na Tutu took up the cause. Between 1994 and 2014, fifteen other states passed consent laws. Several of the states, like California, connected education with medical consent because school districts often require proof of vaccination or other medical records before a child can be enrolled. When states combine access laws, they provide smoother entry into education and care.

The Na Tutu understood that many policymakers weren't aware of their issue—that relatives often raise children outside the child welfare system and consequently have a harder time accessing educational services than parents or caregivers with a legal relationship. With sample legislation in hand, they began crafting a plan to raise awareness of the issue among policymakers.

State Senator Suzanne (Susie) Chun Oakland became one of their staunchest allies. Having served for twenty-six years in the Hawaii State House and Senate, Susie was an anomaly—young and female in a predominately older, male legislature. She recalls knocking on doors early in her tenure, when she was running for reelection. One constituent opened the door and, when he heard who she was knocking on behalf of, said to her, "He's a good man, that Representative Chun."

Susie was known to be calm, centered, and very focused. Deeply rooted in ohana, she remembers growing up in a supportive extended family that taught her not to see barriers, only opportunities. She held the belief that you can make a difference if you don't give up. It was natural for Susie and the Na Tutu to form an alliance. As the chair of the Human Services and Housing Committee, Susie introduced the consent legislation, based on Jackie's research and the Na Tutu's recommendation.

To build support for the legislation, the Na Tutu made *tutu* (grandparent)/*keike* (grandchild) rag dolls out of their own grandchildren's worn-out clothing. They personally delivered a doll to every member of their state legislature. Each doll carried a real-life story of a child, including the barriers that prohibited the *kupuna*, the elders, from enrolling their grandchildren in school and playing a role in their educational plans.

According to Na Tutu member Helen Wagner, for three years Jackie directed the kupunas to show up—not just as concerned grandmothers but as determined voters. They testified before committees, gathered signatures, and persevered. In 2003, the legislation passed, allowing any caregiver who has lived with a young family member for at least six months to sign an affidavit of "caregiver consent" to enroll the child in school and allow the child to participate in curricular and cocurricular activities.

With the stroke of a pen, relative caregivers were no longer frustrated bystanders. By signing the affidavit, they were swearing the child didn't live with them just to attend a certain school or participate in athletics or take advantage of a special program or offering. Unlike many other states, the Hawaiian affidavit didn't have an automatic end date; it was valid so long as the relative was raising the child. Most importantly, while the form had a signature line for parents to sign, if they wouldn't or couldn't sign, the affidavit was still accepted.

The bill was a culmination of years of dedication, research, networking, and learning about the legislative process—a terrific win for the children and their creative advocates in a state with the highest number of multigenerational families in the country.

But the Na Tutu, and other grassroots activists like them, didn't stop there.

Why Education?

Advocates like the Na Tutu begin in their own communities because, as former Speaker of the House Tip O'Neill said, all politics is local. Apart from the Individuals with Disabilities Education Act (IDEA), which is the primary source of federal money for special education services, most control over education happens at the state and local school district levels.

In Hawaii and beyond, the voices of voters raising grandchildren, nieces, nephews, and other children proved the most powerful influencer, changing school district and state laws to help the children in their care. The advocacy groups prioritized education because they knew how hard catching up could be for children whose schooling was interrupted. We see this detrimental impact on children in foster care—who often move school districts when they move foster homes. While the national high school graduation rate is around 87 percent, the rate for youth in foster care is much lower—around 56 percent.[1]

Every student's individual circumstances are unique. Some grandfamilies entering new living arrangements and school systems must create patchwork solutions. "We got the oldest one in school; it was an overcrowded school," said grandfamily caregiver Robert Brown. "They didn't have any school for the middle one, but my wife and sister-in-law, who were in the educational field, tutored him. The youngest we took to a day care at the YMCA."

Grandfamilies living in small towns or close-knit communities may not face the same barriers as others in larger or unfamiliar school systems. "I don't remember my grandparents having any trouble getting me into school or taking me to the town doctor, who was a good friend," said Lance Robertson, who was raised by his grandparents in the 1980s. "It was a small town, and nobody questioned them even though they never had formal custody or guardianship of me."

In many places, if a relative caregiver doesn't have the legal status required to manage the education of the children they are raising, the school can't communicate with them, says Dr. Michael Robert, superintendent of Osborn School District in Phoenix, Arizona.

"We'll do everything in our power to help the grandparent establish that [legal relationship]," he says. "We will have conversations with the biological parent, urging them to give the grandparent [who is raising the child] the legal ability to communicate with us. [We do this] honestly, not manipulatively. I'll tell them, 'All you have to do is say, I allow my mom to be able to access school records and make educational decisions, independent of me being present. It doesn't mean you're giving up on being a parent.' I'll bring out my laptop. I'll type it up for them, get signatures and witnesses, and get it notarized. But if they don't have it formalized, I can't break the law."[2]

States may accept these letters of consent from parents, but if the parents can't be located, relatives may need to prove that they've tried to find them. In some cases, showing that they've tried is enough. In other cases, states may declare the children homeless under the McKinney-Vento Homeless Assistance Act, a federal law providing for the education of homeless children. Because they are deemed "homeless," students in grandfamilies can remain in their current schools or immediately enroll in a new school, even if they don't have the records required for enrollment.

How troubling that grandfamilies must resort to categorizing the children they are raising as homeless in order to get critical services.

Some states focus on a child's best interests for the purpose of schooling, treating the child—and not the parent—as the legal resident of a district. Even then, a grandparent can face another barrier to enrollment if they don't have access to a child's immunization records. This is how a lack of access to health care triggers ineligibility with the education system. The detours and roadblocks result in lost time and frustration for grandfamilies.

Students in kinship foster homes have better school outcomes than students in nonrelative foster placements, according to a Massachusetts study. Those students living with family members had fewer school changes, better school attendance, and lower rates of discipline, and were less likely to be held back to repeat a grade than students in non-kinship homes. The children said they have more school stability, safety, greater chances for involvement in school activities, and are more likely to give their best effort.[3]

While Keonte Jones's parents were a part of his life, he had always lived with his grandma, whom he called "the backbone of the whole family." At age twenty-one, he was preparing to go to college in Fairbanks, Alaska. It was far from his home in Washington, DC, where he lived with his grandma in the Grandparent Apartments, which were built for families with aging caregivers and the children they are raising.

"There's nothing I can do to repay my grandma for everything," said Keonte in a recent interview. "She's been on my team 100 percent, every step of the way, learning about therapists and schools that helped me with my ADHD and anger issues. She has been very supportive and trying to encourage me.

"I found that I excelled in my computer class in high school," he continued. "That was the first A I've had in years on my report card—because it was the one class that I actually took seriously.

"With ADHD, you find if there's something you like, something you're really interested in, you will do anything to focus on it. Now I'm going to go to college in Alaska. I'm interested in cybersecurity, and they have a very good scientific program. I may even be able to work with NASA!"

Keonte embarked on this new phase of his education with hope and plans for the future. "Knowing that I can be fully independent, without relying on my grandmother, is the ultimate goal," he said. "I want to make my grandma, my parents, and the people—the teachers who supported me through all the years of my education—proud."

While children in grandfamilies like Keonte's are more likely to succeed academically than their peers in foster care, they often face serious challenges that interfere with their education. This includes the profound toll of family separation on a child's mental and physical health and the life-threatening risks posed by poverty and food insecurity. More than three-quarters of teachers said in a recent survey that they saw the negative effects of hunger on students' concentration and academic performance.

Language and technology are other possible barriers for relative caregivers who don't speak fluent English or aren't familiar with the online platforms a school uses. Supporting children who have disabilities and special needs—a scenario that's more likely in grandfamilies than in all families—may require even closer communication with a school.[4]

Constance Jones, Keonte's grandmother, recalls how much she missed him when he left for college. It wasn't until she received his late-night call telling her he'd arrived safely in Fairbanks that she could relax. Like other heads of grandfamilies, she gave Keonte the gift of stability so he could succeed in school and pursue his dreams.

Grandfamilies of America Fight for Education in Maryland

In northern Maryland, Pat Owens was determined to get the education and services that her grandson, Michael, deserved. She and her husband raised seven children, including four they adopted. Michael had lived with his grandparents on and off from the time he was born, until finally he came to live with them full-time.

Pat was exasperated by opponents of the educational consent legislation, who falsely claimed that grandparents living in higher-quality school districts would only claim that the children lived with them so they could transfer out of lower-performing schools. This idea of "school shopping" made no sense to Pat and other caregivers, who were worried about harmful delays in the children's education.

As one grandparent said, "We know what to do—just get out of the way and let us raise these kids."

While Pat was fighting for this legislation, she cofounded and became president/CEO of Grandfamilies of America, a grassroots children's and aging advocacy group. With Pat on the front lines, Maryland grandfamilies spent three years doggedly hounding their representatives, as the Na Tutu had.

Pat was nearly sidelined by the school boards for Baltimore City and Baltimore County, which feared a mass exodus to the county from city schools, which had a notoriously bad reputation. (Baltimore City's dropout rate in 2005–2006 was 10.52 percent—the highest in the state, compared to Baltimore County's rate of 4.15 percent and other surrounding counties that came in below 2 percent.)[5]

Like many other opponents of the new law, the Baltimore County schools were concerned about who would pay for these added children, if grandparents in more highly rated school districts were school shopping. That concern has sidelined the education of students across the country—including an honors student who took a bus from Pennsylvania to Washington, DC, to escape his abusive mother and live with his grandmother. When he arrived, officials kept him out of school for six months because he was not a resident of DC, and his grandmother lacked legal custody. She too was accused of school shopping; given the low ratings of DC's educational system at the time that the grandmother was trying to enroll her grandson, though, this was hardly the case.

While the school shopping argument has been raised in several places, it's seldom justified—regardless of the actual quality of the schools. Most grandparents and other relative caregivers simply want to ensure a good education for the children and play a role in making decisions about that education.

Pat and other advocates successfully overcame the opposition by walking the halls of the Maryland State House and meeting individually with legislators to tell their stories of frustration and hope. At the same time, the bill's sponsor worked to nurture relationships with school board members and gain support.

At first, the Maryland grassroots advocates wanted the legislation introduced as a combined medical and education consent bill, like the law that existed in California. They soon learned this could delay passage of the educational consent bill. They agreed to split the bill, which led to medical consent becoming law first.

They continued their advocacy, sharing personal stories of children suffering because they were being kept out of school for weeks and even months. This directly contradicted the school board's threats of penalizing caregivers for keeping children out of school. As this came to light, it became embarrassing for school officials, and in 2005 the law eventually passed and was signed by the governor.

"We just wore the judiciary down in both the Senate and House," said Pat.

Today, Maryland advocates say that the law's implementation has been uneven, with some counties doing a good job and others not. Fortunately, Ali Siegmund lived in a county that embraced the law.

A recent University of Maryland graduate with a BA in psychology and family science, Ali was in her early twenties when she stepped into a parental role for her twin seventeen-year-old sisters, Hannah and Sarah. She had been flourishing at Generations United in her first professional position and settling into a new apartment in Washington, DC, when her widowed mother fell into a coma in June 2022 following transplant surgery.

Pat Owens and grandson Michael at the 2017 GrandRally.
Photo credit: Children's Defense Fund.

The girls' mother stayed in the hospital for eight months. Her daughters didn't know if she'd ever come out of it.

In the beginning, Ali traveled back and forth from DC to the family home on Maryland's Eastern Shore, checking in on her sisters, visiting her mom, and later helping to care for her mother during her long recovery in a rehab facility.

As the teens' senior year in high school approached, Ali's mom was still in a coma and not able to enroll her daughters in school. They were in danger of having their education interrupted right as they were approaching the end of high school, and college application season was beginning. Because Ali learned about the Maryland law Pat had worked so hard to pass, she was able to sign an affidavit declaring that she was the twins' caregiver. She was able to access her sisters' school records and enroll both girls in school on time.

Overwhelmed by her responsibilities, Ali reluctantly quit her job, sublet her apartment, and moved back home as her mother was transitioning from a rehab center to in-home care. Ali wanted to support Hannah's and Sarah's normal teenage activities like prom night, college applications, and high school graduation. She took family photos, planned celebrations, and took her sisters to doctors' appointments, all while their mother was slowly recovering.

Ali remembers going on a college tour with one sister. During the opening orientation, they were seated together with the other parents and students. Then they were separated into one group for students and another for parents. It was an awkward experience, Ali said, since she was only four or five years older than the children of the parents who she joined.

This was just one of many unique experiences she'd have until the twins turned eighteen and came of age to make decisions for themselves.

Ali said she kept her role as "parent" until her sisters didn't need it anymore. She knew it was time when the "How do I do this?" questions started to come less often. She felt different as the relationship shifted from parent to mentor. It was a learning experience, she said. She's grateful that her mom is feeling better and glad to be back in her hometown, living in the house she bought and loves, and enjoying her sisters as sisters.

Given the stress, worry, and uncertain future Ali faced as her mother recovered, she was relieved that she didn't have to fight over access to the twins' education.

Others are not so fortunate.

Even in states where a policy allows a grandparent or other relative to enroll their child in school, some school district officials aren't aware of it. In these cases, the district will reject the request of a relative who is trying to enroll a child.

In Illinois, where Adrian and Joey lived, some grandfamilies were turned away, even though the state statute said that adult relatives without legal custody had authority to enroll children in their care. After learning about the problem, the Illinois Department on Aging helped address the confusion by developing a fact sheet on how to enroll children in school.

The resource was shared at support group meetings like Adrian's Gift of Hope and through other channels, so caregivers could hand over the sheet if they were turned away from enrolling the children. It included this statement from the Illinois State Board of Education:

> Illinois law does not provide any specific requirements for proving residence. It is a question of fact whether a child is actually "in" the district, and not in his or her

> parents' custody or control. A district cannot require legal guardianship. Some districts request, but cannot require, written confirmation from the parent or legal guardian that the child is in the actual custody and control of a non-parent or non-guardian. Districts may request, but not require, a statement or affidavit from the non-parent or non-guardian.

The simple step of showing this piece of paper to school staff can help families like Adrian's get the education their children deserve.

The School as a Safety Net

Schools can serve as hubs of support for grandfamilies by connecting them to services and resources outside of academics. They can help with other ongoing issues, including hunger. School breakfast and lunch programs are another important lifeline, given that one in four grandparent-headed households may not regularly have all the food the family needs. Compared to food insecurity rates among all households with children (15 percent), the need for grandparent-headed households with grandchildren is more than 60 percent higher.[6]

Twenty-six-year-old Nafeis Robinson of Philadelphia said he was grateful for the meals his three younger siblings, ages six, fourteen, and sixteen, received at school. "My mom passed away on December 28, 2023," Nafeis said, "but I've been taking care of them since I was seventeen years old." The children receive free school breakfasts and lunches, and Nafeis provides dinner.

"My baby brother in first grade eats a lot—he eats better than anybody else! He gets way better nutrition," Nafeis said. Even with a full-time job and some financial support, he struggles to keep the refrigerator full. It would be nearly impossible without the meals the three kids get in school.[7]

The trauma many children in grandfamilies have faced, and other challenges and barriers, means that they are more likely to need special assistance in the classroom. Students with disabilities are also more likely to be bullied, which can worsen their trauma and severely affect their well-being and ability to learn.

This is why the Individuals with Disabilities Education Act (IDEA), which funds special education services, is so important. Fortunately for grandfamilies, the US Department of Education regulations define "parent" to include relative caregivers or anyone acting in place of a parent or who is legally responsible for the child's welfare. That means schools should include relative caregivers in the development of Individualized Education Plans (IEPs) for children with disabilities.

Of course, no plan is perfect. The accommodation for Jan Wagner's granddaughter Nessa was to put her alone in what she still calls the "white room," Jan explained in a recent interview. "No windows. A room with nothing in it for her to calm down in.

"You get an aide who's going to grab Nessa by the arm, and then [Nessa's] right on the floor, screaming, continuously violent," she said.

Ultimately, Jan and her husband were the ones to make the accommodation: Jan gave up working.

"Sometimes I'd cry all the way through a support group meeting; sometimes I'd be so angry about all the things I never knew existed," she said. "Working with the intermediate school district, none of that information was ever available. The only reason is because I befriended the foster community."

That's where Jan's advocacy journey began: "I stood there, and said, 'How can you ignore this whole population? How can you not give these families this information?'"

The Power of PIE

It means a lot to children in grandfamilies to have their grandparents feel as comfortable coming to their school as other parents do. In a WBUR interview, Linda Lewis, who is raising two great-grandchildren in Oklahoma City, illustrated this: "I went to the school for Thanksgiving to eat Thanksgiving dinner with my little girl. And I'd fallen last Christmas and broke my femur, so I hadn't been to any school functions or anything.

"When [my great-grandchild] thought I wasn't gonna come, and they pulled me up there in a wheelchair, and she saw me, she began to cry," Linda continued. "And I began to cry. And . . . that was the happiest moment, to see how happy she was just to see me. And I will never, ever forget the look on her face when she saw that her mama was there."

Eugene Vickerson, who raised two grandchildren in Atlanta, shared a similar story. "I would often go in and have lunch with my granddaughter, and she would be so proud that her Papa was there eating with her. She would bring her friends, and her little friends would stand around. And my granddaughter would be so proud to say, 'This is my papa.' Several of her friends asked [if] I could be their papa too. So that same experience was just such a joy, coming in there and giving that special extra love."[8]

For other grandparents, access to school doesn't necessarily translate into active engagement in children's education. Grandfamilies may not feel welcome or see themselves reflected in the world of schools. It may have been years since a caregiver has walked the hallways, visited a classroom, or sat in a lunchroom.

Schools often use language that is exclusively about "parents"—parents' night, parent-teacher meetings—and only occasionally include guardians or caregivers. They may host a "grandparents' day" meant more as a show-and-tell for the occasional, not 24/7, grand.

Annette Saunders, a Baltimore-based grandmother of two, decided to address this omission by founding the country's first Grandfamilies Parent Teacher Student Association (GPTSA). Her unique approach to recognizing and giving voice to grandparents reached another level when, in 2014, she helped pilot Grand Partners in Education, affectionately known as PIE. Funded by the W.K. Kellogg Foundation, the two-year project aimed to tap into the wisdom and energy older adults can bring to helping children in pre-K through third grade learn and succeed.

At the time, Glenmount Elementary and Middle School in the Baltimore City Public Schools district was struggling to engage parents. They realized that with the parents' busy schedules, the grandparents were often the ones taking the children to school. When Annette approached the school about forming the GPTSA and later piloting PIE, the principal was eager to say yes. It was a treat to focus on possibilities for engagement rather than the challenges. PIE was positive.

Annette recruited a steering committee of parents and grandparents at Glenmount to develop the parent involvement plan required for Title I schools (schools with poverty rates of 35 percent or higher). She explained, "Grandparents understand the importance and value of a good education."

Sheldon, one of the grandfathers who participated in PIE, echoed this when he said, partway through the program, "I want our children to have an equal opportunity to succeed in life and have access to a high-quality education. PIE helps me be a part of the process to make that happen."

Some of the changes discussed by the grandparents and school staff involved simple solutions. One grandmother pointed out, "I can't even pick my grandchild up from school when she's sick. The emergency contact form only has room for one name, and the name isn't mine. Is it so hard to add another line?"

The answer was no, and the form was changed.

PIE's family involvement plan named four successful elements to grandparent involvement: brand the project, let families lead, be practical, and start simply.

PIE members also found a creative way to illustrate the importance of why families, including grandfamilies, needed to be advocates for a high-quality and just education for children: Engage the voices of the children themselves.

Curelle Myles, then a third grader, dressed in a plaid jumper with white barrettes in her hair, held a Cinderella lunch box as she took center stage. She gave a moving monologue in the character of young Ruby Bridges, a famous American activist. Using Ruby's voice, Curelle told the story of federal marshals escorting her to New Orleans's all-white public William Frantz Elementary School in 1960. Sitting in the back seat of the marshal's car, her mother told her not to be afraid.

Pushing her pink glasses back up her nose, Curelle, as Ruby, described being greeted at school by people spitting on her and telling her to go away. Without using notes, for close to three minutes, Curelle described Ruby's long first year in a school that didn't want her; she persevered with the support of her family.

Curelle ended her soliloquy proudly saying, "I was the first African American child to desegregate an elementary school." History today credits six-year-old Ruby's bravery with helping to pave the way for civil rights action in the American South.

People loved the presentation, which was repeated at the invitation of the Parent and Community Advisory Board of the Baltimore City Public Schools and taped by the Kellogg Foundation for their archives. It was a lesson in history, a boost to a child's self-esteem, and a bona fide example of the power of family engagement in their children's education.

When the program ended, the final celebration included—what else?—pie.

Support for Learning—at Every Stage

After one of their many court appearances, Adrian took Joey back to his school. It was the middle of the day, and classes were well underway. When they arrived, Adrian walked into the school, expecting to take him to the office to explain why he was tardy once again.

The school staff knew how hard Adrian had been struggling to gain custody of her grandchild—and the many challenges that he faced. This time, when Adrian and Joey opened the school door, they were met by a row of teachers and students who applauded and cheered for them in support when they entered.

Relative caregivers and educators can work together to help meet a child's needs—academic and behavioral, as well as emotional. Adrian's experience is a powerful reminder that schools can be wonderful and welcoming hubs of information and support for grandfamilies, who may feel overwhelmed by a new set of significant demands.

In the summer of 2024, Sarah Smalls, at seventy-eight years old, took time off from work and drove from her home in Virginia to the White House. She and several other relative caregivers were invited to join policymakers and advocates for an afternoon briefing on child welfare transformation and local efforts to address ongoing challenges for children and their caregivers.

Speaking as part of a panel discussion, Sarah shared how she and her husband raised three grandchildren who are now all in their twenties. They were the reason why, she later said, she was still working.

The audience, including Representative Danny Davis, a US congressman from Illinois and longtime grandfamilies champion, listened intently as Sarah and others spoke. In the past, Davis said, his congressional district had the highest percentage of children living with kinship caregivers in the country.

"For these families, extra benefits via Social Security or TANF, however small, can be a lifeline," Davis said. "Supporting kinship caregivers strengthens families and helps children thrive."[9]

He stayed for the entire afternoon, a rare time commitment from an elected official. When he left, he said, "We must do more for these families."

Sarah described how she and her husband decided that they would do everything possible to keep their grandchildren out of the foster care system. She chuckled when she added that they'd do so even if it meant her husband had to sell his luxury SUV for a Toyota Sienna minivan. Their three grandchildren were growing up, playing soccer, and going to events. They needed the extra room the van provided.

Then Sarah shared with the audience the complexity of navigating parenting again, this time in the twenty-first century. When she began talking about education, she

Rep. Danny Davis receiving lifetime achievement award (2009).
Photo credit: Generations United.

offered a concrete example many in the audience could relate to: "You have grandparents raising grandchildren who are attending school," she said. "Math is done differently now. I looked at it sideways and said, 'What?' Who's going to help them?

"You hit a button on a laptop, and something pops up at you," she continued, "so you have to ask your grandson, 'Can you help me with this?'"

As relative caregivers support their children's education, they're also learning.

"We Have All Been Caregivers."

GRAND Voice: Brittney Barros

My four siblings and I entered the foster care system when I was eleven.

My mom did her best, but unfortunately, her addiction and the poverty we experienced were not on our side for us to stay together as a family. At the time, neither my father or stepfather were in the picture. My siblings and I bounced around from foster home to foster home and from group home to group home—the type of residential facility I call modern-day orphanages for foster youth. For a while I lived in one where they would underfeed us: I lost fifteen pounds in one week, and I eventually developed an eating disorder as a result. My family had experienced homelessness in the past, and I was so miserable that I would tell myself every day that I would rather be homeless with my family than living in a group home where the staff don't care about me.

My grandmother would come visit me in the group home, and one day, I was allowed to leave to stay with her for a couple days. As I was getting ready to go for my first home visit, the staff did their rounds, as usual. While cleaning and checking for "contraband," they found a teddy bear under my bed. Claiming that my room was messy, they wrote out a loss of privilege, which meant I couldn't go for the visit.

It was traumatic, and it was a pattern. Yearning to live with my family, I told the judge about my grandmother and about how loving, caring, and kind she was. I advocated for myself, saying that if I was able to move in with her, I would be free of the abuse and neglect I'd experienced in the foster system. The judge agreed that I should be where I call home—with my grandmother, instead of the caseworker. After many years of being a ward of the state, my time in the foster care system finally ended! I was able to go back and live with my grandmother. She eventually got guardianship over me and my younger sister, who came to live with us soon after.

My grandmother has always been my inspiration. As a single mom, she worked at General Motors for thirty-five years. She built her own house, and despite her adversities, she always took care of herself and those around her. She kept the house clean and even painted it every year so it would be in tip-top shape. She instilled many of the values that make me who I am today, including being kind to others and loyal to those closest to you.

Most importantly, my grandmother taught me unconditional love: She didn't have to take us in, but she did. She did everything she could to make sure we had a loving childhood despite the trauma we all faced. She also taught us to stick together and support one another.

Less than a year after I moved in with my grandmother, she was diagnosed with dementia. She also began developing an eye condition called macular degeneration that led to almost blindness, and she could no longer drive me to school and appointments. For a few years, I ended up taking care of her, with the help of my younger sister, to make sure she was fed and clean.

Eventually, Adult Protective Services got involved, and they deemed my grandma unfit as a guardian. I was a legal adult by then, but not old enough to be my sister's guardian. My grandmother went into a nursing home, and my sister went and lived in different homeless shelters for teenagers. I continued my studies, pursued a competitive internship, and settled into work. When I was twenty-one, I got legal guardianship over my sister, and my brother emancipated himself from the foster care system in Missouri.

When my sister lived with me, it was a rough time for both of us. She lost her father—my stepfather—and struggled with mental health challenges and behavioral issues. Some of her disruptive behavior caught the attention of my neighbors and then my landlord. I was given an ultimatum: Either she goes, or you both do. Worried that I would lose my Section 8 housing and we would both be left homeless again, I was forced to give my sister back to the system. Luckily, my little brother was able to gain guardianship and care for her in my grandma's house.

In my family, we have all been caregivers. It's not just my grandmother taking care of me, or my taking care of her. It's also my sister taking care of my grandma, my brother taking care of my sister, me taking care of my sister. We've had these kinds of handoffs over the past five to ten years.

My grandma was a badass warrior. There are always trials and tribulations and pain, but by speaking out I'm turning my pain to power, to policy. It's my way of honoring her.

For that reason, and because of the traumatic barriers that I faced in the child welfare system, I've dedicated my entire personal and professional life to bettering it. I've completed a bachelor's and a master's degree in social work, with a concentration in welfare of children and families, from the University of Michigan, as well as a second master's in public policy with a concentration in social policy. My career goal is to become a program evaluator for services within the child welfare system so that I can influence federal policy. With that in mind, I'm now working toward my PhD in social work and social welfare, also at the University of Michigan, so I can fulfill this dream. I currently work with the Michigan Supreme Court and the Michigan Department of Health and Human Services, running a program I created called the Youth Advocacy Project. We hire youth champions—professionals with lived experience in the system—to help children in foster care navigate their court proceedings and family team meetings and authentically engage in defining their future.

Given my negative experience with foster care, I want to make sure young people have an opportunity, if they cannot go back with their bio parents, to be able to stay with family. Kinship families are where young people can thrive and be their best selves—connected to their cultural background, their heritage, and their familial ties themselves.

Though I got a full-ride scholarship for my undergraduate degree and my two master's, I have $32,000 in student loan debt. That's because, while my grandma is in the nursing home, I've had to pay the mortgage and electricity bill and take care of my siblings. It's a challenge, but I would do anything in the world for that woman; she doesn't deserve to have her home go into foreclosure. Eventually, when I have the money, I want to have her mortgage paid off and her house all cleaned up and made ADA compliant, so she can come home where she belongs.

That's how much I'm willing to invest in my grandma because of what she's invested in me.

CHAPTER FIVE:

Everything Was an Immediate Need: Financial and Food Insecurity

> "I tried to appear at friends' houses around dinnertime so they would include my grandchildren in the dinner. They got so they would eat pretty much anything, even if they didn't like it."
> —Alice Carter, grandfamily caregiver who raised two grandchildren[1]

Stacey Walker was a star from a very young age; in 2006, as a high school student, he was selected as National Youth of the Year and served as a national spokesperson for the Boys & Girls Clubs of America. He was just twenty-eight years old when, in 2016, he became the first African American to ever hold the position of county supervisor for Linn County, Iowa, the second-largest county in the state.

His continued success seems even more profound considering how young he was when his life was shattered—and how much trauma he, his sister, and his grandmother shared as a result.

"Things were tough psychologically for my grandmother," said Stacey, who was interviewed while working as a program coordinator for social innovation at the Case Foundation. "Here she was trying to come to grips with the murder of her daughter and adjusting to the fact that she would once again assume a parenting role for two very young kids."

Things were tough financially, as well, he said. "My grandmother already lived in a government housing project, and although her salary had been enough to keep her afloat, she now had all sorts of new expenses: clothes, food, toys—all the basics any young child needs, multiplied by two."

Caring for loved ones of any age is costly—especially in the United States, where high food, health care, and housing costs keep so many people on the edge of financial security. About half of all Americans have less than $500 in their savings or checking accounts.[2] Two out of three adults who are regularly saving for retirement worry that they'll have enough, according to AARP.[3] Poverty disproportionately affects older adults of color. The share of older Black (17.3%), Hispanic (17.4%), and American Indian or Alaska Native (17.4%) adults with incomes below poverty was more than double the share of older white adults (7.7%).[4]

Most grandfamily caregivers are experienced household financial managers; they just don't have enough to stretch when they take on raising their grandchildren.[5]

Even if the caregivers are working, they most certainly will have to take time off for childcare and other immediate needs. Adrian worked for an orthodontist—an understanding boss. She heard many stories from members of her support group who weren't so lucky.

"A lot of grandparents go to court. Some of them lost their jobs because of so many times in court," she said. "If you're working in a retail business, they need you there. Or even a doctor's office—they need you working because they've got patients or clients coming in that need help."

As a result of these challenges and many others, the number of grandparent-headed households living below the poverty line is 17 percent compared to 11 percent of older adults living without young relatives.[6]

"Everything was an immediate need," said Sonya Begay during a 2020 StoryCorps conversation with her granddaughter Kayle Eppele.[7] Sonya took in Kayle and her two siblings (then ages nine, eleven, and thirteen) when her son passed away. "I had a house that was big enough, but I needed beds, I needed food, I needed to figure out how to get to school and to buy clothing for three kids.

"I had myself, and that was it," she continued. "We spent everything that I had, we spent my retirement, but we got everything together, we got everybody clothed and fed."

Grandfamilies' needs vary widely, depending on the caregivers' assets and the children's challenges; they represent a broad economic spectrum. Generations United has worked with grandfamilies that include the former head of a national foundation, who, along with his wife, could afford to raise his two teenage granddaughters on Cape Cod without needing to find additional support for the family. Our network also included one part-time school custodian who raised a highly special needs infant, struggled to find support, and wasn't shy about saying something.

That custodian, the grandmother of Shaheed Morris, had less than a fifth-grade education. "[My grandmother] had no car, so she used public transportation to get me to therapy every day for almost a year," Shaheed said. "Her income was not enough to keep up with the expenses of a baby with special medical needs. Still, she found a way to piece together the support she needed."

The added responsibilities and costly changes related to housing, legal fees, education, and more can often push grandfamilies into a lower economic bracket and cause them to reach retirement with no savings.[8] Families with lower incomes also face systemic challenges that can make it that much more difficult to break the intergenerational cycle of poverty.

Relative caregivers must forgo their own financial dreams to care for their children. For people who have no retirement savings, the new caregiver role—as essential as it is—can erode a sense of financial stability at a crucial time.

I'll never forget the way one grandmother acknowledged the challenge. "I'm making it. Well, not making it, but I got my head above water," she said.

"Thank God I know how to doggy-paddle. Because if I didn't, I would have drowned a long time ago."[9]

A Seat at the Table for Grandfamilies

Financial stress related to caregiving was a national focus in 2000, when Senator Chuck Grassley and eight bipartisan cosponsors introduced the National Family Caregiver Support Program (NFCSP) Act. The bill focused on middle-generation caregivers helping their parents who are ages sixty or older, as well as other relatives of the same age. Among the cosponsors was Oregon Senator Ron Wyden. A longtime aging advocate, Senator Wyden began his career as cofounder of Oregon's Gray Panthers, a group formed in 1970 to address ageism and other social justice issues.

From Generations United's perspective, the legislation was the perfect opportunity to include grandfamilies and begin moving parts of our agenda forward. Credit goes to Janet Sainer, the tenacious visionary who lobbied for grandparent caregivers to be included in the White House Conference on Aging.

As the bill made its rounds in the Senate, our team made the case for why grandfamilies should be included in the act during a Senate hearing. We argued from a strength-based perspective: Older adults may be the recipients of care, but many are also caregivers. The five-minute testimony was compelling enough to win the support of Maryland Senator Barbara McCloskey and others on the committee, who said they'd never heard of the issue before. The momentum in favor of grandfamilies was growing.

On November 13, 2000, through the reauthorization of the Older Americans Act (OAA), the National Family Caregiver Support Program became law—including grandparents and other older relatives raising children. It was a key victory: For the first time, aging policy recognized grandfamilies and included a provision that could provide services and support for children in their care.

The language included in the law, drafted by Generations United's Ana Beltran, clearly defines the relationship as a grandparent or step-grandparent of a child, or a relative of a child by blood or marriage, who is sixty years of age or older. This person must live with the child, be the primary caregiver of the child because the parents are unable or unwilling to do so, and either have a legal relationship with the child or raise the child informally.[10]

"Raising the child informally" is the critical element in this definition, enabling people who raise children outside the foster care system and/or without a legal relationship to qualify for services provided by the NFCSP.

The law has evolved over the past twenty-five years. In 2006, Generations United succeeded in advocating for lowering the age to fifty-five from sixty, which increased the percentage of eligible grandparent-headed families by almost 20 percent.[11]

The True Cost of Another Mouth to Feed

A grandmother whose resources are stretched thin may joke about doggy-paddling; chances are that when a child entered her life, she was already swimming furiously. A growing number of relative caregivers are aged sixty or older; they're often grappling with traditional aging issues like increased medical costs, accessing Medicare, and stretching their Social Security income.

About 44 percent of relative caregivers are not in the labor force—a proportion that significantly increases among caregivers over sixty.[12] Many live with diabetes, high blood pressure, or other health conditions that make full-time work difficult, if not impossible. They are trying to stretch dollars, spaces, and time to keep their families together.

Nikki Johnson-Huston remembers the grandmother who took her in and raised her. Nikki's grandmother, who had a disability caused by a bus accident, applied for social services and did everything she could to give her granddaughter a "normal" life.

"My grandmother got less money than a foster parent would have gotten," Nikki said. "She got the minimum food stamps and welfare. We had a more robust safety net around us because she was elderly and disabled. And she could stretch a dime in a way my mother never could. She had age and maturity, and I got the benefit of that."[13]

Caregivers still in the workforce can struggle to manage their jobs with additional family needs. Some may be growing in their careers but forced to cut back on hours to balance new demands at home. Others leave their jobs because they lack reliable, affordable childcare. (Only 17 percent of low-income working relative caregivers receive childcare assistance.)[14] When a married couple takes in a grandchild, it's not unusual for one of the grands to stop working to care for the child.

Grandfamilies who form suddenly often stagger under the sudden expenses related to raising children—an average annual cost topping $29,000.[15] One grandmother reflected on buying replacement clothes for her teenage grandson every six months: "Seems like every time I turn around, I am spitting out money."

Grands continue to carry these expenses as the children enter young adulthood. Many children who have turned eighteen (or are about to turn eighteen) still require financial assistance, as they are in college or in jobs that don't pay enough for them to live independently. This is true for Adrian's grandson Joey, who has had his grandmother's support through community college and low-paying jobs since he graduated from high school. She has often said that she doesn't mind. Like many grandfamilies, Adrian and Joey remain deeply connected, even as he has transitioned to adulthood.

Joey joined his grandmother at a 2010 event at the National Press Club in Washington, DC; he even stepped onstage after Adrian finished speaking. The quiet, skinny, dark-haired kid answered questions about his family and told a story about a recent Sunday morning when he fed the dog and cat and brought his grandmother coffee and the paper in bed, telling her she could have an easy day.

When asked why he did such a thoughtful thing, he said, "She works a lot for me and does a lot for the family. I'll pay her back one day, so I might as well start now."

Different Relationships, Different Rules

Six months after Victoria Gray and her husband took in their four-month-old granddaughter, they received a call about the birth of the baby's brother who, they were told, was also their son's child. A few months after the boy was placed in their home, they got another call: "We were told [that] he was not biologically linked to our family, and in order to keep him, we would have to become a licensed foster family," Victoria said.

The difference in the support they received for the unrelated boy, compared to the related girl, was staggering: "After getting licensed, we received $500 a month for him," Victoria said. "We were receiving $17 a month for my granddaughter. So now I'm wondering: What is the difference?"

After all, as Adrian often says, "Those sneakers cost the same, whether or not the child is in the system."

Grandfamilies raising relatives within the foster care system receive a monthly stipend, which differs by state and number of children. Those raising relatives outside the system receive little to no support—and often struggle financially.

For these grandfamilies, their sole source of public support is child-only Temporary Assistance for Needy Families (TANF). This payment considers the need of the child based on the child's own, limited income (from child support, etc.), and not from the family caregiver's income. It includes monthly cash to help meet a child's typical needs. TANF may also include short-term help for one-time expenses such as buying a crib or paying an overdue utility bill. Grandfamilies who receive TANF can also more easily access other support, like Medicaid.[16]

Still, that payment is less than half of what nonrelative foster families receive, and almost always insufficient, covering only a small fraction of the expenses of raising a child.

Jan Wagner said that she and her husband "worked our butts off to keep above water" after taking in their granddaughter Nessa. They were unable to qualify for the types of reimbursement received by friends who raised children through the foster care system. "We fell on some serious health and financial issues, so we had to go through the basic welfare door and apply for Medicaid and food stamps and things like that.

"That was the only way we could do it," she continued. "My foster family friends just laughed: 'Please, you have to go right through the [welfare] door?' Right."

The barriers to receiving TANF begin with the application itself. "It was long and difficult to navigate with language that was not clear," said Victoria.

A huge downside to TANF is that it decreases if a family is seeking support for more than one child. "While the foster care maintenance payment for two children would be double, the TANF payment for two would only go up incrementally," said Generations United's deputy executive director, Jaia Peterson Lent. "Caregivers have joked that TANF policymakers must assume that the second and third children don't eat as much as the first."

This disparity makes keeping brothers and sisters together particularly challenging for relatives. If a grandfamily has received funding to help another child, that history can work against them. Applying for assistance also gives the state permission to first pursue the parents for child support—a process that both complicates and considerably delays the funding.

"If the biological parents had already used that time, then they would consider what they call the grandparent penalty," said Victoria. "We were not allowed to get that money."

A relative caregiver's long-held assets, which, in any other context, might be considered a strength, can be a drawback for families seeking immediate assistance. "[People] are essentially penalized for responsibly saving for retirement or even owning a car," she said. "Even after our family went from two incomes to one income, we did not qualify."

Ultimately, Victoria did what so many grandfamilies do: "We used our credit cards, savings account, and some of our 401(k) retirement funding to care for our grandchildren," she says.

Because of these hurdles and more, only about 13 percent of eligible grandfamilies receive TANF.[17]

Victoria, through her involvement in an informal, statewide support group called Arizona Grandparent Ambassadors, started a program for monthly stipends for grandparents. She went on to found Grey Nickel, which has a program, KinshipHelp55, that helps connect kinship families with support and resources within two days of the child going to live full-time with a relative.

"I now use my voice to support kinship across Maricopa County in Arizona," Victoria said, "so no other family will suffer the abandonment and the financial burden that my family did to help support our grandchildren."

Social Security and Grandfamilies

Social Security is a lifeline for older adults. More than half of US citizens aged sixty-five or older in the United States say that the benefits represent half—or more—of their income. It's less understood that the program can be equally vital for young people in need.

In 2023, 6.2 million children lived in a household that received Social Security as part or all of its income.[18] Several years ago, researchers determined that without the program, the estimated 18 percent of grandfamily households living in poverty would be closer to 59 percent.[19]

"[My grandmother, my sister, and I] barely made it financially," said Stacey Walker, in a 2008 speech before a crowd of grandfamilies. What saved them, he said, were the Social

Security survivor benefits the children received after their mother died.

Social Security was also essential support for Gail Engel, who was working in 2006, when she and her husband took on their newborn grandson. Gail received disability benefits, and when her grandson turned nine, the couple adopted him; as a result, her grandson received a small Social Security payment. "This made a big difference," Gail said. "Finances were always tight, but it eased the burden when he received Social Security as well."

Those payments increased when Gail fully retired at age sixty-five and again when her husband retired. "Retirement can be a challenge for any aging adult," she said. "If you have quit your job to care for family or didn't work in a high-paying career, Social Security may not be adequate. Add a child to that equation, and you have a new budget to consider.

"We couldn't have made it without Social Security," she continued. "We would have had to sell our home."

Another caregiver from Maine, living with three grandchildren and a developmentally challenged adult son, lost her apartment and began moving her family to one motel after another. "I have Social Security, and my son has Social Security Disability Insurance," she said. "Without that, and assistance from the town, Adoptive and Foster Families of Maine, Inc., and the Kinship Program and various other charities, we would be on the street."

The 2011 National GrandRally focused on the power of Social Security to protect children and lift families out of poverty. Handmade signs dotted the Capitol grounds. Two children's signs read "What If It Were Your Grandchild?" And "Social Security—Don't Cut My Lifeline." Caregivers' signs included "Your Cuts Hurt My Bottom

Line," "Focus on Care, Not Cuts," and the simple "Save Social Security."

That day, as the crowd on the Capitol's West Lawn quieted, the first speaker, Morrisella Middleton, explained the essential role Social Security had played in helping her raise her two grandchildren, who had come into her care when they were three and eleven years old. Morrisella's son, their father, had died of a work-related illness, and because of his contributions, the children qualified for survivor benefits.

After caring for her grandchildren for several years, Morrisella was diagnosed with congestive heart failure, malignant hypertension, and cancer. She had to go on disability. Shortly thereafter, during the Great Recession, she then lost 80 percent of her savings, forcing her to rely completely on Social Security.

Morrisella Middleton and grandson (2006). Photo credit: Generations United.

"Social Security has been my lifeline—my only lifeline," Morrisella told the crowd. "It's been critical for me in raising the children and to their future. Thank goodness for the survivor benefits for the kids and what I contributed in the forty-four years I worked. It's been my only token to get by."

Morrisella closed her speech with her own powerful bottom line: "Social Security benefits made the critical difference in my ability to support my grandson rather than leave him to be raised by others."

Table for Three, Dinner for Two

Food is one of a household's biggest expenses, second only to housing. As a result, many grandfamilies facing financial hardship experience food insecurity, defined by the USDA as the "limited or uncertain availability of nutritionally adequate and safe foods, or the limited or uncertain ability to acquire acceptable foods in socially acceptable ways."[20] This dire situation has particularly harmful short- and long-term effects on growing children.

One out of every four grandparent-headed households experiences food insecurity. That is more than twice the national rate.[21]

Families adapt any way they can to survive. "Sometimes people would give us food that had been in their refrigerator for two weeks, but it was better than nothing," remembered Alice Carter, who raised two grandchildren. "Someone gave us a bag of oranges, and we ate nothing but oranges for four days."[22]

Michelle Singletary, who was raised by her very frugal and proud grandmother, "Big Mama," says that her grandmother refused any stipend to supplement her nurse's aide salary. She only acquiesced to help for the children's food and health care.

"She was an amazing person—a very simple person, but in her simplicity, just had a brilliance about money management," Michelle said in a *Generations United* podcast. "She never apologized for what she couldn't give us. We had food on the table. May not have had a lot of extra food, but we had enough. We didn't have a whole closet full of clothes, but we had enough.

"That's my message to grandparents: Don't apologize for what you can't give them," she continued. "Nothing will ever make up for their missing parents. And so why even try? Just appreciate what you have given them, which is security, which is priceless. Priceless."

Grandfamilies in need can get help with their groceries through the federal government's Supplemental Nutrition Assistance Program, or SNAP (formerly known as "food stamps"). Some families raising young children may also qualify for the Special Supplemental Nutrition Program for Women, Infants, and Children, or WIC, which supports children up to age five.

Unfortunately, as is the case with TANF, less than half of low-income grandfamilies' households receive SNAP.[23] Often families don't know whether they may qualify; they may not see themselves in the outreach materials created to encourage families to apply, which often reflect traditional families, not theirs. If they are aware of the program, they may think that the limited benefit they would receive is not worth the trouble.

"WIC was very, very helpful—the kids got cheese, milk, beans, tuna, and fresh vegetables, too, at one WIC store," said Oklahoma-based grandfamily caregiver Linda Lewis. "But that ended at age five. And their SNAP benefits didn't increase when the kids lost WIC. There was nothing to make up for that, and the kids just eat more as they grow."

Linda's Social Security income counted as income for the children; as a result, their access to benefits was limited, she says. "And now the SNAP payment increase we had from the pandemic is gone." Like many relative caregivers, she supplements her family's food options by visiting food pantries once a month and receiving meals from Meals on Wheels.

Some of these barriers could be addressed if SNAP had the flexibility to include a "child-only" benefit, so access would be based on the child's income as opposed to the total household income and assets. Children shouldn't go hungry because their caregivers saved for retirement.

During the COVID-19 pandemic, grandfamilies often struggled to find food. The challenge also shined a stark light on the need for joint meal program support.

"We had grandparents who would take a child to pick up a meal for the child, but they couldn't get one for themselves," said Generations United's deputy executive director, Jaia Peterson Lent. "We had programs that would deliver meals to older adults, but not a meal for the child who was standing beside them in their living room.

"We need to realize that a family is a family," she continued. "We should be able to feed them and support them as a family and not as separate individuals."

In 2021, amid the pandemic, Pennsylvania Senator Bob Casey introduced legislation to address hunger among children living with relative caregivers. "The COVID-19 public health and economic crisis has only further exacerbated the devastating reality of food insecurity," he said. "With so much uncertainty in all other aspects of their lives, these children should not have to worry about when or where they will receive their next meal."

Sen. Bob Casey speaking at the 2017 GrandRally. Photo credit: Generations United.

Food insecurity is about food quantity *and* quality. Eugene Vickerson was sixty-two, comfortably retired, and relaxing on the porch of his home in Atlanta when a strange car pulled up in his driveway. The engine stopped, and a very aggressive social worker from the Division of Family and Children's Services (DFCS) opened the car door, asking for Eugene by name.

When he responded, the social worker retrieved a basinet containing a sixteen-month old granddaughter Eugene didn't know he had. She told him if he didn't keep the baby, they would put her in protective services.

This is how they were introduced. Eugene said yes.

When he looks back on the day, what bothered him the most wasn't his granddaughter; it was what came with her. Potato chips and a soda. The social worker handed these to Eugene in a bag, saying this was her "food." The response of the plant-based advocate? "Man, we don't eat stuff like that. That is not food. That is not food."

"That part is really emotional," he remembers, looking back. "I was so angry and hurt because of the way they handled it, you know—and no previous notice. Not given anything but a half bottle of pop and an open bag of chips."

"My granddaughter was asleep the whole time," Eugene said. "It reminded me of slavery, when they just took the children. I felt like they treated her like a piece of meat."

Eugene is also raising his grandson, though he stepped into a primary caregiving role for him more gradually. When Eugene's daughter would forget to pick up her son after school, Eugene would get the call, and he always came. A night here, a night there became a week that grew to be a month. Because he arrived at a later age than his sister, Eugene's grandson's junk food diet had already been established.

"My grandson's mother had given him a lot of fast foods and unhealthy snacks like french fries and soda," Eugene said. "My grandson has ADHD (attention deficit hyperactivity disorder). I told him his ADHD was part of his superpower. I tried to plug into that and see the benefit of that extra energy. It was difficult to keep him away from sugar, which made his hyperactivity worse. He wanted to eat like his friends."

When it comes to food, Eugene says, "You have to look at it as if you're trying to save your grandchildren. You're trying to keep them safe in terms of food, in terms of what's on the table. If you look at it like that, I think you come up with some different ideas and a different intensity and sense of urgency."

His advice to other grandparents? Start the children you raise on healthy eating when they are young, so it's what they are used to: "It was so easy because that's how I eat, and she ate what I eat," he said. "We ate salads, hummus, pumpkin seeds, and other stuff, and she loved it. She always loved it. You know, children usually eat what they know, and they eat what their parents or caregivers eat."

It Takes a Village

By sharing advice—and challenges—in community, relative caregivers can overcome obstacles in ways they may not have imagined. Support groups can source and offer direct support through a variety of donations, which is essential when direct financial aid is unavailable.

In 2004, Jesse Williams was an eighty-two-year-old full-time caregiver for her seven-year-old great-granddaughter, Dorese, whose mother passed away during childbirth. Rather than bemoan her situation, Jesse emphasized her blessings: She connected with a grandparent support group called Grandparents Offering Love and Discipline (GOLD), which met once a month, offering information, socialization, support, and networking for grandfamilies.

Jesse described the group as a big family. "The first time we got together, we just cried a lot," she said. "It helps to have someone to talk to."

One of the Williams family's key struggles was the astronomical cost of food and school supplies for Dorese, on top of the cost of medication for Jesse and her husband of sixty-five years, who had recently been diagnosed with cancer.

"When I saw [GOLD], I jumped!" she said. "The support group tells us where we can get free lunch for the kids and money for school supplies." GOLD also assisted with housing concerns and transportation to doctors' appointments and the support group.

Many organizations working with children and families have created traditions that support children in foster or kinship care in a fun, stigma-free setting. The San Antonio–based South Texas Alliance for Orphans organizes Grand-Marts and KinMarts—free back-to-school shopping experiences at a church on the north side of the city. Thanks to donations from individuals, nonprofits, and businesses, each child gets a free backpack and "money" to shop for their own school supplies.

"The bottom line is: How can we support these families when the government doesn't want to?" said grandmother Mercedes Bristol, who helped organize the event. The church, she says, is just one example of the many places that can support children and families in need.

"You know, the Church says, 'Thou shalt take care of the orphans and the widows,'" Mercedes said. "And so, we're reaching out to them and saying, 'You know, we are the widows. These orphan children don't have parents. And the community is stepping up.'"

In Smithville, Tennessee, a town of about five thousand people that's about sixty-five miles east of Nashville, the median household income for a family is $30,000.[24] Since 2006, this rural community has embraced Fiddlers Annex, a row of eight apartments for grandfamilies resembling a roadside motel at the end of a cul-de-sac.

The local Lions Club donates frequently, and one of the food banks delivers food directly to the complex. The families' favorite is a Smithville church that, each year, buys gifts for Christmas and invites the grands in to "shop" for their grandchildren. Rides are arranged, and the grands are never late. Once the gifts are selected, church volunteers wrap the gifts, and the caregivers go home toting the bundles they know will bring smiles to the faces of children of all ages on Christmas morning.

"Old Man Wisdom."

GRAND Voice: JJ Hitch

When my sister Toni was six, she packed a suitcase of clothes and another of toys, got on her bike, and pedaled two blocks to the house of our grandparents, Daniel and Margaret, just outside Detroit. She left me and my two brothers behind, where we lived with our father, who abused alcohol and the two eldest brothers.

It was a violent, chaotic household. Toni had reached her breaking point. She didn't have to say anything; I knew she was not coming back.

It didn't take me and my brothers long before we followed her. We were all welcomed by our loving grandparents, who did their best to care for us and give us a sense of safety that our parents couldn't. Adding four kids created a warm but overflowing house that only had three bedrooms for seven people.

You can imagine the impact our arrival had on my grandparents. My grandpa was seventy-two at the time and had worked at Chrysler for forty-four years. He had planned to retire with the package he was offered but had to postpone his retirement for another five years. My grandmother was sixty-two and still working the midnight shift at a fast-food chain.

Suddenly they had complete responsibility for four kids. I was fourteen and the oldest; Toni was the youngest. The expenses were incredible. My grandparents had to buy bedroom furniture, clothes, and food for us. Their income was very limited, so it was extremely difficult for them.

Our father protested us kids leaving, so Child Protective Services got involved. They determined the home we'd run away from, our parents', endangered our well-being, so they formally placed all four of us with our grandparents.

Unfortunately, as the caseworkers began their home visits to my grandparents' house, they saw what they considered to be a hazardous living situation that didn't meet foster care licensing standards. They threatened to take us into custody.

The problem was that while my grandparents' house was safe and filled with love, it didn't have enough bedrooms or bathrooms to meet the state's criteria.

My grandpa loved nature. He had bought ten acres before we came to live with him and had been building his retirement house there. With the state pressuring him and my grandma, the need to finish the new house accelerated. My uncle helped by teaching us to lay the hardwood floors, and we all did everything we could when we weren't in school.

I was in high school at the time, and it was a four-year blur in flight mode to survive. When the state would come to inspect the house that we were scrambling to build, there was always something that needed fixing. The standards were designed for strangers in foster care—not a family. The handrails, the blinds, the paint on the walls, and the grout on the tiles; the red tape of the system needed to be completed before we could enjoy the love of that home.

It seemed so shallow to me when my life was in danger. So, we'd go back to pulling all-nighters to try to fix what the system found unsuitable. We didn't want to be taken away and either split up between different foster homes or worse, placed back with our parents, who still had the same problems we'd left behind.

Construction costs and meeting our basic needs meant my grandparents were spending more than they could bring in. One time they were six months behind on the house payment and were told they'd be evicted.

My grandparents were forced to file for bankruptcy. We all felt responsible. It ruined their credit.

For years, my grandparents struggled to care financially for us and recover from bankruptcy. The house they built created a home base for us.

Three of us went on to do well. Toni graduated from high school, and one of our brothers went into the military. The other one didn't do so well.

I joined an organization called FosterClub and became a young activist advocating for changes in foster care. I spoke at one of the national GrandRallies in Washington, DC, and shared a poem I'd written for other kids who'd had experiences like mine. It was a message of hope.

Working with other advocates, we were successful at changing laws, but I knew I couldn't wear that youth badge all my life. I went on to get my master of arts in communication, the first person in my family to get a college degree.

I worked in eye donations, and now I'm in tissue procurement. I'm creating a silver lining out of death. I know what I'm doing helps someone. It feels good when I hear from someone who's benefited from my work. That makes me feel whole and complete.

I miss my grandpa. He eventually passed away in his comfortable chair with his kitty on his lap under his left arm. I will always have the memories of peace and long conversations with him. He taught me all he could—eat better, think better. You know, old man wisdom with an occasional dirty joke!

He is the one who connected us to nature and a life that pays forward. I hope he knows his sacrifices weren't in vain. Grandpa made so many things happen for us. He's always the voice there with me. I'm always trying to think the way he did.

Being able to connect and love nature makes the biggest impact on me. I'm still healing from injuries. Nature is where I go to find peace. I thank my grandpa for teaching me to get in tune with nature and the courage to continue to grow in the ever-changing world.

CHAPTER SIX:

Going to Grandma's House—and Staying: Housing Challenges

> "I love Michelle and Denise to the moon and back. They are my life. I can look toward [their] future because of this community where the girls are safe and we have a home with so much love around us."
> —Rita, grandmother, Oregon[1]

Olivia Chase says the silver lining to a family life clouded by the impacts of mental illness and crime is that she gets to raise her grandson, Richard. According to Olivia, a fifth-generation Washingtonian and resident of the Plaza West Grandparent Apartments in DC, Richard's father, her son Oliver, or Ollie, as she called him, "wasn't college material, so he joined the army." He came back from his tour of duty in Iraq with "wounds you couldn't see," she said. He suffered from post-traumatic stress disorder (PTSD). Olivia asked the military to help, but they said not to worry; he would be fine.

Before he was deployed, Ollie married a woman whose life wasn't on the trajectory that Olivia, a retired nuclear medicine technologist and community activist, wanted for her son.

Following his return from Iraq, Ollie and his wife moved to Texas. On a night when Olivia said Ollie's mind was "messed up, and he wasn't thinking straight," he and his wife, who was pregnant with Richard, tried to rob a "gambling house," believing the patrons wouldn't call the police.

They were wrong.

Before the police arrived, the couple killed a man in the house and escaped back home to Washington, DC. Soon after Richard's birth, they were arrested and extradited to Texas, where Ollie is now serving a life sentence and his wife fifty years in prison.

Richard was just three months old when he came to live with Olivia full-time. She'd sold her house earlier and downsized to a one-bedroom apartment, which was fine when he was a baby.

Olivia Chase and grandson Richard (2018). Photo credit: Generations United.

When Richard first arrived, Olivia instinctually offered love and care. She wasn't thinking that a three-month-old would turn into a three-year-old, a thirteen-year-old, and so on. But children change, they grow, and by the time Richard had become a rambunctious eleven-year-old, she felt like her apartment had shrunk.

Olivia said she knew it was time to move when the living room of her tiny apartment became a parking lot for a bike and a skateboard. "I'd get up in the middle of the night to go to the bathroom, and you know, it was a little dangerous!" she said.

Around this time, in 2018, Plaza West Grandparent Apartments opened with fifty apartments for grandfamilies in Mount Vernon Triangle, one of the fastest-growing zip codes in DC. Olivia and Richard were among the first families to move in. While she says that "Richard is the air I breathe," she knew she needed a little more room to breathe. Moving into a two-bedroom apartment, she had it.

Plaza West's brick apartment building sits on a triangle of land with a view of a major thoroughfare on one side and the city on the other. Olivia and the other grands love the location, access to buses and shops, and, until recently, an urban Walmart. It has a fenced-in, locked outdoor space with enough room for picnic tables, play equipment, and, perhaps sometime in the future, a community garden. The "concierge" is a guard at the front desk in the lobby. Only tenants and their guests are allowed in past the locked gate and secure lobby entrance.

Unlike typical affordable senior housing, the first floor of Plaza West includes a playroom, gym, computer lab, and a small room for morning coffee chats or grandfamily support group meetings. It is bright and light throughout, though the most stunning room is the top-floor community room, with its wall of windows looking out on the city. It's the site of holiday parties, town halls, community meetings, and more.

Grandfamilies rave about having a laundry room on every floor and a bedroom for every child. Olivia said that one of her favorite parts of living at Plaza West is that when she and Richard need space from each other, they can find it. Her eyes lit up when she said, "And I don't have to talk kid talk all the time."

Richard continues to grow, and even the two-bedroom apartment is beginning to feel small. He no longer fits in a twin bed. He's now taken over the living room as his bedroom. Olivia said she doesn't entertain much, so she doesn't mind.

Room in the Heart, Not in the Home

Today there are at least nineteen specialized grandfamilies housing projects across the United States. It's not enough. One of grandfamilies' major challenges is the high cost of housing. While they aren't alone in this experience, they are impacted at a higher rate than many other families. In 2023, a little more than 31 percent of American households were considered "housing burdened," meaning that they spent more than 30 percent of their monthly income on housing.[2] Among lower-income grandfamilies, almost half spent more than 50 percent of their monthly income on housing. Less than one out of every three income-eligible grandfamilies receive housing assistance.[3]

Housing can be even tougher for American Indian and Alaska Native grandfamilies who live on tribal lands. They have much higher incidents of problems with plumbing, kitchen and heating, structural deficiencies, and overcrowding than the general grandfamily population does.

When Robyn Wind, a citizen of the Muscogee (Creek) Nation, brought home her three-month-old grandson, he was in delicate health, having been on a feeding tube. As the Oklahoma weather topped 90 degrees, Robyn's air conditioner stopped working. When she reported it to the tribal housing program, they challenged her, insisting that the unit's fan still worked. It took five years for them to fix it.

Adrian said that housing is one of the top issues faced by the families in her support group, Gift of Hope. One grandparent, who joined the group when she became responsible for raising her two grandchildren, lived in a senior-only subsidized apartment, meaning that her lease banned children from living there. She found herself telling her grandchildren to be quiet all the time.

That grandmother lived in fear, Adrian said. Whenever there was a knock at the door, she gave each child a cookie and put them in the closet. Eventually she was caught, and her worst nightmare came true—she was evicted. One system said, "They are yours"; another said, "You are on your own."

This isn't unusual. Children often come into the care of relatives unexpectedly; grandparents and other older relatives may have downsized to a smaller home or moved to an age-restricted community. Others may be living in small government-subsidized apartments that prohibit anyone else from living in the same apartment—and certainly not someone who is "underage."

Subsidized housing run by local housing authorities may not recognize the new grandfamily as a "family," which requires additional space. This is especially true when the caregivers don't have legal custody of the children. They face being put out on the street with little notice, whether they plan to seek custody or not.

For these reasons, the grandfamily apartment buildings that do exist, while not perfect, are treasured by the families.

The first housing in the nation built for grandparents and the children they are raising was the GrandFamilies House, which the nonprofit Boston Aging Concerns, Young and Old United opened in Dorchester, Massachusetts, in 1998.

"I took [my granddaughters] when I came over here to look at the apartment," shared one grandparent for a report, "Life at GrandFamilies House: The First Six Months."[4]

"They lay down on the floor, 'Oh yes, yes. We're home,'" she continued. "They just couldn't wait to get in here. They went and told all their friends in school: 'A mansion. We're like the Jeffersons. We're moving on up.'"

Boston Aging Concerns, Young and Old United influenced future developments by transparently sharing what they got right and what they'd do differently if they had the chance.

One lesson they learned was on architectural design. The complex was built with child safety and aging-in-place features, and with windows facing a central playground, so grandparents could watch the children from the comfort of their apartments. Still, they missed the mark on other design opportunities. An open two-story atrium looked good, but it was also a dream come true for children who loved to climb up the guardrails and look over the ledge. It was soon retrofitted with barriers to dissuade young explorers.

They also recognized the need for supportive services on-site, help with issues facing children and aging caregivers, and the enforcement of boundaries with visitors, including the children's parents.

Seven years later, after studying the accomplishments and setbacks of the GrandFamilies House, the first new ground-up construction for grandparents raising grandchildren, PSS/WSF Grandparent Family Apartments, opened in New York's South Bronx.

This is where Dorothy Jenkins and her grandchildren moved in 2005.

Dorothy is always impeccably dressed and jauntily wears her "church lady" hats. These are not subtle barrettes or nondescript, floppy straw chapeaus; hers are an African American woman's crown—the kind you wear to church on Sunday to praise God.

Her smile is patient. She'd raised her children to successful careers and was called back into parenting duty when her daughter, whom she called the light of her life, started using drugs—something Dorothy never understood.

She said she had no other choice.

When her daughter died of a brain aneurysm, Dorothy, recently widowed, was still grieving for her husband. She took in her three grandchildren, ages eighteen, twelve, and two. It was a daunting task, but she says she did it because she loved her daughter. She still looks at her picture on the wall when she gets up every morning and aches.

After her children were grown, Dorothy had a plan for the life she wanted to live. When she retired, she was going to buy the biggest car she could find, put on a pair of jeans and sandals, and drive across the country. She said she would have thrown her hat in the back seat because she's a hat-wearing grandmother.

Instead, she retired early to look after her grandchildren, getting them to school, graduations, and appointments.

"I don't know where I put my dreams," she said during an interview on NPR's *News & Notes*.[5] At the time of the interview, her youngest granddaughter, Brittney, was "acting good," Dorothy said. Brittney was the spitting image of her mother; seeing her made Dorothy think that her daughter was still alive.

When Dorothy moved into the Grandparent Apartments, she became the voice for the tenants. She came to Washington, DC, to testify about the value of the apartments and the on-site services. When then-Senator Hillary Clinton, considered a rock star by many grandfamilies, came to the apartment building's community room to announce new legislation she was introducing, Dorothy was there to greet her.

Dorothy's development has fifty apartments (forty two-bedrooms and ten three-bedrooms) in a six-story,

Dorothy Jenkins and Sen. Hillary Clinton (2006). Photo credit: Generations United.

66,470-square-foot building. The building and its apartments were designed for older caregivers, youth, and children. The hallways are wide, and there are emergency buzzers in each apartment, handrails in the bathrooms and hallways, laundry facilities on each floor, and downstairs community space with separate rooms for the grandparents, teens, and young children. This is where comprehensive on-site services are offered, including educational before- and after-school activities, support groups, and case management. To keep the building safe, there is twenty-four-hour security, including staff at the front desk verifying identities and cross-referencing visitors with court orders.

Life for grandfamilies looks very different in Smithville, Tennessee—an unlikely place for one of only two federally funded national grandfamily housing demonstration sites. (The other is in Chicago.)

When Fiddlers Annex opened there in 2006, the organization struggled to identify grandfamilies to fill the eight two- and three-bedroom apartments. Two obstacles prevented needy families from moving in—the 62+ age requirement, as grands are more likely to be younger, and the rural location. Living in a rural area would be a tough shift for grands who were used to stepping out their door and finding everything they needed within a few blocks. Most importantly, the area lacked access to health care. The town of Smithville had few medical professionals and only one small hospital to serve the aging caregivers.

Grandmother Crystal says she loves it there, though, and wouldn't trade her new home. She moved into her three-bedroom apartment in 2024 and marveled at the space she had for herself and her three grandchildren, ages eight to seventeen. She most liked that she fit in—something she hadn't felt in other places where she'd lived. "The grandparents here help each other," she said one day as she was sitting on the front porch, passing time with another grandmother. Together, their homes were the apartments' "bookends," with Crystal on the far-left end and her friend on the far right.

What Fiddlers Annex missed in local amenities, it made up for in easy housing transition options. Fiddlers Manor, a larger senior-only apartment building, was just one street away. When children graduated from the annex and left home, the grandparents could move easily into the manor and stay in their familiar neighborhood. The adult children would get jobs and find their own place to live or go off to college.

This was the case with Chloe, who was raised by her aunt at Fiddlers Annex. When Chloe was accepted into Vanderbilt University and became the first in her family to go to college, the teenager whom the staff of the Relatives as Parents Program described as "a little adult" didn't have the clothes—or the money to buy clothes—to wear there. The compassionate, practical staff went beyond their job descriptions, going through their own closets to put together outfits that would help Chloe feel confident as she started her life's new chapter.

Once Chloe arrived at the university, she took a selfie every morning in a new outfit and texted it to her aunt, who shared it with the staff. Vicki Durham, head of the Relatives as Parents Program for fourteen counties in rural Tennessee, smiled when she remembered how good it felt each day when she opened the new picture.

LEGACY: Building the Foundation for Grandfamily Housing

The funding that made the Tennessee apartments possible had an inspiring, film-based beginning. Shot over a five-year period, the 2000 Academy Award–nominated *Legacy* tells the story of how members of one African American family faced the murder of their teenage grandchild and brother, broke free from welfare, overcame addiction, and escaped the violence in their community.[6]

Legacy was produced, directed, and written by Tod Lending, a documentary filmmaker who views his art as an opportunity to fuel social change. It chronicles the Collins family, who, for four generations, were trapped by poverty, depending on welfare, and living in one of the oldest and most notoriously dangerous public housing projects in America—Chicago's Henry Horner Homes.

The film, narrated by granddaughter Nickole Collins-Pierre, shows the family's struggles, successes, and relapses as they seek to escape the specter of violence in their community.

Then-fifteen-year-old Nikki states, "You have to believe in yourself. You have to depend on yourself, because you know where you want to go. No one else knows where you want to go but you." She is determined to achieve something in life. "Believe in yourself," she says. "If not, you will not survive." Nikki's strength is rooted in her emphasis on the essential value of self-confidence and in the support of her extended family.

Dorothy, Nikki's grandmother and head of the household, plays a central, stabilizing role, helping to raise Nikki and several of her other grandchildren. The strong intergenerational relationships, in addition to Dorothy's dedicated mentorship, keep the family together and moving forward in the face of setbacks and obstacles that might derail them.

Legacy was used in outreach and education for hundreds of communities. The goal was to inspire discussion and action around a wide range of topics such as drug abuse, life skills and career development, trauma and grief, and grandparents raising grandchildren. In addition to motivating community action among professionals and caregivers, the film inspired the introduction of legislation in 2001 entitled LEGACY—Living Equitably: Grandparents Aiding Children and Youth—to assist with alleviating intergenerational family housing needs.

Screenings of *Legacy* around the United States, often followed by panels featuring members of the family, inspired groups of viewers to launch letter-writing and call-in campaigns to their members of Congress. They asked the representatives to sign on as cosponsors or to support LEGACY in other ways.

The film ends with Nikki's graduation from high school and her grandmother moving the family into a new home away from the projects. In the years that followed, Nikki graduated from college—the first in her family to do so—and went on to teach in the Chicago school system, marry, and start a family of her own.

Nikki played a pivotal role in LEGACY becoming law, speaking at the first GrandRally in Washington, DC—the same 2003 rally where Adrian found her people. The timing couldn't have been more perfect. The day before the rally, an amendment was offered in the Senate to include provisions of the LEGACY bill in the American Dream Downpayment bill, President George W. Bush's housing priority. LEGACY, which had been introduced in 2001, now had a good chance of becoming law.

Two months after Nikki spoke at the GrandRally, LEGACY was signed into law, providing a possible funding stream for safe and affordable housing for grandparents and other relatives raising children. It did so by creating national demonstration projects to develop housing specifically for grandfamilies, such as Fiddlers Annex; combating misinformation by providing training for federal, state, and local housing staff about grandfamilies; and calling for a national study of grandfamilies' housing needs. The legislation authorized funding elder housing with a $10 million set aside from the Section 202 Supportive Housing for the Elderly Program.

To celebrate, Generations United gave personalized bricks to the champions on Capitol Hill, thanking them for "laying the foundation for intergenerational housing."

However, just because funding was authorized didn't mean it was granted. The Department of Housing and Urban Development (HUD) didn't implement the law until 2005, when Michigan Senator Debbie Stabenow led the charge to appropriate $4 million. While she was inspired by the first rally, where she spoke and also met Nikki, Senator Stabenow's support was sealed by one constituent in Detroit. A single person who voted in her state.

Every week, this advocate would call Senator Stabenow's office and leave a message with her staff, asking her to sign on in support of LEGACY. The combination of persistence on the part of a vocal voter and Nikki's inspirational story moved the senator to support the bill and later become the main champion for funding its provisions. The following year, appropriations bills provided $3.96 million for "Section 202 Demonstration Program for Elderly Intergenerational Families," also known as LEGACY. The remainder was used for the study and training outlined in the law.

The LEGACY Act sunsetted, or phased out, in December 2008, five years after it was enacted. It didn't end, though.

The HUD appropriations bills for fiscal years 2021 and 2022 each included $10 million set-asides for LEGACY—the only funding for intergenerational housing that the department ever made available.

It's not enough money to come close to meeting the housing needs of grandfamilies. The application guidelines for the funding are onerous. So complicated that, in fact, one year none of the applications reviewed met the requirements, and the funds sat dormant while the demand stayed steady. There should be a straighter path leading to a grandfamily's home.

Help Building a Home

Building new multifamily housing is only one part of the housing solution. Sometimes families need help retrofitting an existing home they own, like JJ Hitch's grandparents did. To accomplish this, some grandfamilies depend on relatives and loans. Others lean on local repair services or housing programs.

This was the case for Jaylan Gray when, over the course of a couple of years, both of his parents and his grandfather died. At age twenty-two, Jaylan was left to raise his twelve-year-old brother Julian.

Jaylan promised his mother just before she passed that he would take care of Julian and keep him in their family's house. "[I] try my best to keep him in check, make sure he doesn't get in trouble, and make sure he's loved," said Jaylan.

But it wasn't easy. The house their mother left them in Katy, Texas, was severely damaged by Hurricane Harvey and other storms that left it flooded and in deep disrepair. A contractor swindled Jaylan out of the $20,000 he had for renovations and left the home in worse shape than he'd found it, punching holes in the walls and taking the air conditioner. Trying to honor his parents' wish and raise his brother in the home they'd always known, Jaylan was devastated.

Katy Responds, a local volunteer organization dedicated to restoring and rebuilding homes for families, stepped in and completely renovated the home, free of charge, in about three months. A local church furnished it just in time for Julian to begin the new school year living in the place he'd always known and going to his familiar school. Thanks to the kindness of strangers, this grandfamily was able to stay in the home their mother left them and maintain some stability as they navigated their lives without parents or grandparents.[7]

There are different versions of these kinds of handyman programs in many states. Organizations like Habitat for Humanity and Rebuilding Together provide home repair services for low-income homeowners, prioritizing repairs that will improve the health and safety of their residents. Some programs at the community level are government-funded; others are faith-based, relying on sponsors and donors.

Commonsense Housing Standards for Grandfamilies

The important regulations put in place to keep kids safe in foster homes, such as provisions for separate bedrooms and access to indoor plumbing, make no sense at all when applied to grandfamilies. Neither do certain square footage requirements and obligations to have private, outdoor play space. Instead, they become barriers for grandfamilies trying to remain in or secure safe and affordable housing.

In many families, it isn't unusual for siblings to share bedrooms. Some Native American grandfamilies on tribal lands lack indoor plumbing. For JJ Hitch's grandparents, adhering to state foster care guidelines drove them into bankruptcy.

Had the National Model Family Foster Home Licensing Standards been available then, and had the state adopted them, it would have been okay for JJ and his brothers to share a bedroom. But they weren't, so he and his siblings would come home from school and work with his grandparents trying to bring the house up to foster care requirements.

Eventually—after much remodeling, paperwork, and financial stress—JJ's home qualified, and his grandparents became licensed foster parents. They received financial support for their grandchildren, though still not as much as someone unrelated would have been given to care for the children.

In 2014, advocates concerned about families like JJ's, who were just trying to do the right thing, worked collectively to create licensing standards for family care. These model standards remove common barriers that would have benefited JJ's grandfamily and not impacted the children's safety. Some of the adjusted rules address the strict mandates. The "bedroom" requirements are replaced with "sleeping space" language, which allows for children to sleep on their grandma's sofa bed or in bunk beds, provided other children in the home are treated similarly. In the case of rural families, the standards allow for drinking water to be well or bottled water and do not require bathroom facilities to all be in one room.

In 2019, the standards were adopted, and many states have moved quickly to enact them, making it easier for families around the country to bring the children they love home, where they belong.

"Most people go to [their] grandma's house and get spoiled, but for me it was the only safe place I had," Chad Dingle remembered. "Getting to live with Grandma was like 'going to Grandma's house' all the time. I had more love there than anywhere else in my life."

"I Always Had the Essentials."

GRAND Voice: Shaheed M. Morris

I was born on April 12, 1988. A few days later, my mother got dressed and walked out of the hospital, leaving my care to the hospital staff. At the time, my father was incarcerated. My father's mother came to the hospital and was given two options: Either someone from the family had to claim me, or social services were going to get involved.

Looking back, as I reflect on my grandmother's life of giving and helping, it's not much of a surprise that she would step forward to take custody of me. Nana was a loving lady who provided for her family, including her disabled children who lived with her. She had already raised one grandson, as my uncle was deceased.

This arrangement was only supposed to be temporary, but my mom never was able to wean off the drugs. What should have been a short period of custody turned into a lifetime.

My mother went into labor on her front porch, as my grandmother told the story, and she was drinking heavily while in labor. She told me the paramedics moved the bottle from my mother's mouth after loading her onto the stretcher.

When I asked my grandmother why they all didn't try to stop her from drinking, she said that when you're dealing with people with addictions, you can say anything you want. They could have tried everything, but it fell on deaf ears.

I was born very small, and at first, they didn't really realize how sick I was. As days went on, it became clear: I was born with fetal alcohol syndrome and addicted to crack cocaine. The prognosis was grim. I couldn't move my neck. I wasn't expected to live. My grandmother was told that if I could receive the necessary therapy, I might be able to regain movement in my upper limbs.

She knew the gravity of the situation. During my first year, she rode two buses, five days a week, to get me to physical therapy. Thanks to God and advancements in medicine, I am alive, without any physical or mental health challenges.

Nana had a strong work ethic. She was born in the Jim Crow South and moved north as a teenager for economic opportunity. She started out working in the laundry room at Trenton's St. Francis Medical Center and then worked for the Trenton Board of Education for twenty-five years. She raised eight children with a fifth-grade education and a custodian salary.

Since 1965 she had lived in Trenton's Miller Homes, which the local paper called the Killer Homes. It was a very violent housing project. When there was an asbestos leak in 1995, we were able to move out. She bought a modest home on Pearl Street for $39,000.

Sometimes my grandmother's income wasn't enough to keep up with our expenses, but I always had the essentials. I never went without food. While asking for help wasn't easy for someone so strong-willed, she did accept WIC for me. I never came home to find there was no running water or electricity, as some of my friends had. I had the stability of staying in the same school my whole life, while some of my friends were constantly moving.

I began taking college-level courses at our county's community college shortly after graduating from Trenton

Central High School. I transferred to South Dakota State University, where I received a bachelor's degree in journalism and finance. I worked in television for one year and hated it. Then I moved back in with my grandmother and went to mortuary school.

I've always been around funerals. With Nana being older, she knew more people, and more people who had died. I remember going with her to funerals when I was as young as five. One of my childhood dreams was to become a funeral director. My first job was at a funeral home, cutting grass, when I was fourteen. I love helping families during such challenging times.

My mortuary college graduation was my grandmother's first time ever on a college campus. By then, she was living with congestive heart failure. I knew how sick she was when she let me sweep the floor for her. I took time off from work to care for her.

There was nothing I could do to prevent the end of life from occurring, but I wanted it to be as peaceful as possible. She passed away in 2021, at the age of ninety-four.

After she passed, I learned that there was a reverse mortgage on the house. I was able to buy it in a short sale; in six months, the house was in my name. Her children who are disabled are still here. I don't know if it's my forever home, but I'm here for now.

Through that process I became interested in real estate. While working full-time, I began managing properties on the side. Now I'm working as a public information officer for the New Jersey Housing and Mortgage Finance Agency. I'm taking online courses through Iowa State University, working toward a master's degree in real estate finance and development.

As an emerging developer, I want to provide housing for grandparents who are raising grandchildren.

I stand here as living proof that supportive grandparents in the lives of young people can help them overcome challenges—even the tough challenges I faced. They can take an infant whose birth diagnoses and life may have appeared hopeless, and they can serve as a transformative figure in the life of that child.

My mother and father were never in my life; I did not receive a single gift from either of them. But my grandmother had a big heart and a generous spirit. She was always there for me.

EPILOGUE:

Living Grand: Building the Future

> "Growing up with a childhood full of trauma and abuse, there were very few moments where I felt safe and very few people with whom I felt protected. Being put into my uncle's care was the best decision that could have ever been made for me. It wasn't an easy road by any means, but I have no doubt that it completely saved my life."
>
> —Kindra, raised by her uncle, Bob Ruble

When I first met Shaheed Morris in 2016, he was in a suit, exuding confidence with an undercurrent of nervousness and vulnerability. Such a contrast to most kids raised in foster care. Instead of owning suits, many of them have owned foster kids' suitcases—plastic garbage bags filled with their clothing and few belongings, which they are given the day they age out of the system.

Instead of facing life on the streets, Shaheed stood proudly, a big guy who couldn't be missed, waiting for his turn to speak before an audience of advocates and policymakers in a Senate office building on Capitol Hill. It was one of the first public events organized to sound the alarm about the opioid epidemic, the latest in a long history of substances

Shaheed Morris speaking on Capitol Hill in 2016. Photo credit: Generations United.

that have torn families apart and left children to be raised by relatives.

At the time, Shaheed was an aspiring journalist, so he was thrilled to be introduced by columnist Michelle Singletary, who was also raised by her grandmother. They shared a connection of deep love for the kin who cared for them when they were young.

When Shaheed took the floor to tell his story, the reception chatter went silent.

As he spoke, I found it hard to reconcile the picture he painted of the lifeless baby he was when his grandmother stormed into the hospital to rescue him and the well-spoken, high-functioning adult before me.

I thought back to my first year working at Generations United and the Capitol Hill staffer who said to me, "The apple doesn't fall from the tree. Why should we help these people make the same mistakes with another generation of children?" I smiled when I remembered the grandmother who contradicted this argument during a Hill briefing, saying, "We don't throw away any of those apples that are damaged when they fall. We make apple pie, apple juice, apple jelly. So why would we throw away a child?"

Under other circumstances, Shaheed could have been tossed aside, living with untreated, severe disabilities. Or he could be dead. He told me later that his grandmother saved his life. Because of her determination and the lessons he learned from her, he has two college degrees and is now working on a third while pursuing a master's degree in real estate finance and development. He's also a licensed funeral director in the state of New Jersey, an avid runner, and a healthy food fan. His desire to help others is strong.

Every day, Shaheed wakes up in the house that was his Nana's, the home where he slept growing up—the home he now owns. He's renovated it and carefully maintains it, as his grandma had before him. It is still his place of refuge.

Shaheed is a living testament to the powerful role grandparents, aunts, uncles, and other relatives play in loving and raising children whom others might cast aside.

It's not just Shaheed who's succeeded because of a grandparent's love. JJ Hitch spoke with me about the battle he remembers between being a child and trying to help his grandparents meet state standards for housing—and feeling like the standards meant more to the caseworkers than his stability.

He is still healing. The COVID pandemic and his brother's posts overseas prevented his sister and brothers from seeing each other in person for a long time. That's changing now.

In December 2024, they celebrated their first Christmas together in a decade. Between them they brought spouses and five children—soon to be six, since his sister Toni was

JJ Hitch, center, with his sister and brother. Courtesy of JJ Hitch.

pregnant with her third child. They are starting their own traditions and, he proudly told me, "We're sharing laughter and not drama. We're in a healing place."

Like Shaheed and JJ, Adrian's grandson, Joey, could have had a much different life. Given his parents' inability to raise him, he would have gone into the child welfare system if his grandmother had not fought for him. If his trajectory had followed many kids in foster care, he could have experienced multiple short stints in strangers' homes. Foster parents are often caring strangers, but if he were raised in the system, he never would have known his roots and family stories.

Joey would have lost ground on his education and not received the care and coaching he needed to overcome his special needs. He most likely wouldn't have finished school, let alone gone on to begin learning skills he could use to support himself independently. He might have ended up in the same position as approximately twenty thousand foster kids who age out of the system every year: no family to return to and no couch to crash on.[1] They often face homelessness with little hope for the future.

Joey never would have had someone to call Babi.

"Grandparents and other relatives are our nation's best natural resource when it comes to making a difference in the lives of vulnerable children," said Senator Ron Wyden at the 2017 GrandRally. "[They] are often the first to step up and take care of the children who are left behind."

Because of the love, sacrifice, and unfaltering devotion of Adrian, other family members, and extended family, Joey, and hundreds of thousands of young people like him, have warm memories behind them and rich lives ahead. They need to be seen, celebrated—and supported.

From Few to a Field

All the families you've met in these pages, with their individual successes and unforgettable stories of resilience, represent but a few of the millions of unique grandfamily stories. They've stood strong as others judged them, and they've felt buoyed by a compassionate network of people who believe in what grandfamilies can achieve with even just a little bit of assistance.

At the first GrandRally, Adrian was impressed to learn that grandparents and other relatives save taxpayers more than $6.5 billion a year. She'll be even prouder when she learns the latest estimate is $10.5 billion a year.[2] In addition to serving as an essential familial and social safety net, grandfamilies have generated a groundswell of compassion and meaningful change. New and revised public policies have created pillars for a platform of support for grandfamilies. This is an important starting point for future generations to build on.

Today, support groups and other grandfamily-focused programs, many run by kinship caregivers themselves, operate in every state and in many communities.

In Generations United's work over the years, we have seen how the relative caregivers in our network find both the support and the motivation to do the same for others. Those individuals often become the new leaders, continuing to push for additional changes and collaborations to build stronger grandfamilies now and in the future.

Adrian's first GrandRally led to her starting dozens of support groups in Illinois, meeting with the governor and policy staff, and testifying before local officials. Not bad for a shy grandmother who never gravitated to the spotlight.

Child welfare systems are now required to give more effort, not just lip service, to finding family members to take in children when their parents can't raise them. Compassionate child welfare workers are more likely to have the tools and feel emboldened to spend more time searching for little-known branches of a family tree.

Some states are implementing innovative practices. New Mexico now has a Kinship Unit dedicated to searching for, contacting, and assisting family members, providing training and engaging other kin to help create an extended network for the grandfamily. Missouri created "Extreme Recruitment" to identify kin using staff and a private investigator. Other states are also finding innovative ways to walk the talk of seeking out family members first.

Had family finding been a common practice when Sixto Cancel was growing up in foster care, his caseworkers would have discovered that he had an aunt who lived fifty-eight miles away from him, and who would have adopted him along with the four unrelated children she did adopt from foster care. Instead, he bounced from foster home to foster home until he aged out of the system at twenty-three.

Six years later, when Sixto was twenty-nine, his sister invited him to a family reunion, where he was introduced to family members he'd never met, including his aunt.

"I will never forget that I could have lived with people who loved me," he has said.

In 2015, Sixto, a bright, charismatic social entrepreneur, went on to found the nonprofit organization Think of Us, a research and design lab working to transform child welfare, pioneering the use of technology to build better outcomes for children. When he appeared in a "Brief but Spectacular" segment on *PBS News Hour*, he said, ". . . without the human beings who are in our life to be there to guide us, how much opportunity do we really have? Recent laws and legislation allow for us to do things differently. Now child welfare is able to actually provide services without having to separate a family."[3]

Progress Needs Protection

Just as no child is born with a user guide, children placed with relatives seldom come with referrals or resources to ensure the newly formed family succeeds. Grandfamilies are left to figure it out on their own.

Thankfully, kinship navigator programs, federally funded in each state since 2014, are helping to fill the information void.[4] These resource centers are a place where grandfamilies can learn about helpful state and local programs and policies. Early navigators in states like New Jersey, Ohio, and Washington proved they were a cost-effective, efficient method of providing vital information to kinship families. This led Generations United and other groups to advocate for federal support for the programs. Funds were modest but enough to help states get started. In 2018, we were successful in securing ongoing federal funding for programs proven effective and the first six years of funding for state navigators to develop or improve their programs.

Unfortunately, at the time I am writing this book, federal funds are being severely and indiscriminately cut, jeopardizing federal government funding for kinship navigator and other programs.

Still, we fight. Testifying before a Senate Finance Committee meeting in 2024, GRAND Voice Laurie Tapozada asked for continued support for kinship navigator programs and closed by saying, "Please help us to do the important stuff—raising our kin children to be happy, healthy adults with a strong sense of self and family, who can be self-sufficient and successful. Our work is not easy, especially for us grandparents . . . But we do it, heart and soul."[5]

Another significant change came about when states were given the flexibility to establish grandfamily-specific foster care licensing standards. Several states and tribes were quick to begin adopting and implementing these more family-friendly standards, which don't take shortcuts on safety but do allow family members the flexibility to share rooms and make other accommodations. This is a game changer for grandfamilies who faced the same hardships that JJ's faced trying to retrofit a home to meet unnecessarily strict standards.

Most importantly, states are required to ensure that licensed or approved kin foster family homes receive the same foster care payments as non-kin foster homes. None of the old second-class treatment for kin.

GRAND Voices Advocating for Change

While awareness of grandfamilies has grown incrementally over the past few decades, it wasn't until Casey Family Programs supported the creation of Generations United's GRAND Voices Network that policy and perception changes shifted into high gear. The staffing and training GRANDs receive is critical, but even more important is the affirmation and connection they bring to each other. It takes courage to share intimate stories abundant with personal pain, and, as one GRAND said, "I know now I'm not alone."

In recent years, GRANDs have been instrumental in making sure that grandfamilies who formed because of the opioid epidemic were included in three state opioid settlement plans. They were overlooked in the federal language, but their tenacity is paying off where it's most important—state implementation. We provide the tools and talking points; they provide the heart and passion.

Keith Lowhorne, our GRAND in Alabama, was the first to be successful. Three Area Agencies on Aging (AAAs) serving twelve counties in the state were identified to receive $270,000 as part of a pilot that, if proven effective, could go statewide. Keith said the legislator he was talking with called when it passed and said, "Give me some slack now that we got it started."

With Keith's reply, "Politicians are supposed to have thick skin!" he warned the policymaker that he'd be back. He believed $270,000 was the first money to support grandfamilies, but it definitely must not be the last of the nearly $100 million Alabama has received from the opioid settlement.

For Generations United and our GRANDs, it's a reciprocal, respectful partnership. As one GRAND responded when we surveyed the network, "I'm very grateful and thankful you have given me this opportunity. I hope to be a light to all I serve."

Other examples of their impact are abundant. In 2023, GRAND Victoria Gray testified before a House subcommittee hearing on Temporary Assistance for Needy Families (TANF), sharing why proposed work requirements would be unfair to grandfamilies. Her testimony led to praise across the aisle, including near the end of the hearing. "You are all wonderful people," said Ohio Representative Brad Wenstrup about the witnesses, "but, Ms. Gray, I don't think I have met a living saint in my life, but you are right up there."

One essential lesson we've learned over the years is to never underestimate the strength and resiliency of a GRAND. Inspired by their impact, Generations United is designing a Youth Voices program as a parallel project to amplify the perspectives and stories of young people like Shaheed, JJ, Brittney, and others raised in grandfamilies. The GRANDs have shown how such storytelling can make a significant difference. This work is also one of our core strengths.

Sarah Gesiriech was instrumental in helping Senator Grassley understand the importance and long-term value of grandfamilies. Later, when she got to the White House as a member of the Domestic Policy Council, she continued to champion the families. In 2002, she advised that President George W. Bush's declaration for National Family Week include in the proclamation "Many single parents, grandparents, and others also raise their children in difficult circumstances, and these dedicated individuals deserve our respect and support."

The Kids Are Alright

The young people raised by grandparents and older relatives are amazing. The obstacles they've overcome, the trauma they've experienced, would have crippled less resilient souls.

"If they hadn't fought for me to stay with family and stood up for me every step of the way and, frankly, sacrificed a comfortable retirement for me, I would be in a very different, and I think much sadder, place," said Adam Otto. "This spring, my husband and I celebrated our third wedding anniversary. I have two adorable cats, a vibrant friend group, and I bought a home last year. That wouldn't have been possible without them."

Their past experiences may differ from their peers, and, as a result, they may have unique ways of seeing the world. This does create challenges, but also many benefits.

"My grandparents understood that kids need stability, discipline, and a steady pattern," Lance Robertson told me. "We had to get up every day at 5:30 a.m., even on the weekends. We'd bale hay and do other things once my grandpa retired, and we moved to the country. Even on days he didn't have chores for us, he'd make something up."

When Lance turned seventeen, his grandfather took him to breakfast—a gesture that he assumed was a birthday gift. "Then we went to a strip mall where all the branches of the military had recruiting offices," he said. "He looked at me and said, 'What's your choice?'

"I was surprised and said, 'Wait, don't I have a say in this?'" Lance continued. "My grandfather said, 'Yes, you do—you have a say in which branch.' Because of the way I was raised, when I went into the army, it was a piece of cake!"

A young policy champion on our staff was raised by her great-grandmother, Granny. While other young people her age are out clubbing, she likes nothing more than going home to a quiet house and crocheting. She is patient and listens. She is also whip-smart, valued on the Hill as much for her policy acumen as her ability to share her firsthand experience.

A former staffer who was raised by his grandparents loved to do puzzles and play board games—all very different hobbies than his contemporaries. Rather than partying on a beach, he enjoyed cruises with his grandmother.

Relative caregivers shine when they reflect on the success of their adult children. When they learn about someone raised in a grandfamily who became an Oscar-winning actor, the head of a major corporation, a well-known singer, or even the president of the United States, they remember the sacrifices are worth it. Hope blossoms in their hearts for the children they love and have helped survive and succeed despite the odds against them. They realize the crucial choice they made—to say yes to a child and navigate the challenges that come along—was the right one for every member of their grandfamily.

Twenty years after the 1995 White House Conference on Aging, where grandfamilies were first introduced to the national spotlight, invited guests were welcomed to the 2015 White House Conference on Aging by a man raised in part in a grandfamily. That man, President Barack Obama, said:

> "My grandmother was a fiercely independent woman. She helped to raise me. She didn't have a college degree. She worked her way up . . . until she was vice president of a local bank. And after my grandfather died, she chose to live independently. And Medicare and Social Security allowed her to make that choice. . . . That was a promise this country made to her and all its citizens. And as a grateful grandson—who happens to be president—that is a promise I'm going to make sure we're going to keep for future generations."

Just another grateful grand success.

Joey is grateful, too, though now he prefers to be called Joe. He's been to junior college and is working while continuing to live with Adrian. A gift for them both. Adrian, now 85, misses her mother, Double Babi, who lived to be 101, and her husband and best friend, Ron. Joe and other family members, along with the grandparents she continues to lift up, give her life hope and purpose.

As Adrian ages, she and Joey continue to cruise together. This time, though, it's Joe taking her to the doctor and other appointments. And like Adrian, Joe says he wouldn't have it any other way.

Wes Moore and grandfather, Papa Jim. Courtesy of Joy Thomas Moore.

AFTERWORD:

Governor Wes Moore

A grandfamily was part of my life long before I knew it had a name. And I am who I am because of it.

I was not yet four when my father tragically passed away. I remember in those early years in Takoma Park, Maryland, how my mom struggled as a young, single mother of three. Not only did she lose her best friend, but our primary support system as well. When it became overwhelming, Mom took my sisters and me back to her childhood home in the Bronx—the home where she came of age, embraced by the supportive and loving arms of her parents. Despite its diminutive size, the house became our refuge and my grandparents our surrogate protectors—the direct link to our ancestral past.

My mom was a journalist, which allowed her to find writing jobs across New York City. This required long and irregular hours away from home and working late into the night while at home. My grandparents provided my sisters and me with the stabilizing presence needed to keep us grounded.

My "Mama Win," with her lilting Jamaican accent, shared stories of her life in Cuba and Jamaica while teaching me her favorite West Indian dishes. An elementary school teacher of forty years, she supervised homework time when my mom was not there to make sure it was done. My grandfather, affectionately called "Papa Jim," was one of the most humble and spiritual men I have ever known. His roots were deeply embedded in the church. His father came to the United States from Jamaica to study divinity. Upon graduation, he took his young family to South Carolina, where my grandfather was born.

However, those were the days of Jim Crow, and my great-grandfather became a vocal critic of the growing popularity of lynching. When he learned that he himself was on a hit list, he took his young family and fled back to Jamaica in the middle of the night. My great-grandfather vowed never to return. But his son was determined to claim his birthright, and he enrolled in and received his degree from Lincoln University—and later seminary. My grandfather would grow up to become the first African American to be ordained in the Dutch Reformed Church, the previously sanctioned religion of apartheid South Africa.

Those years I spent with my grandparents, and watching my mom work so hard to make a way for us to attend the best schools and have the most opportunities, showed us the value of multigenerational families. My sisters and I learned never to be afraid of challenges, no matter how formidable. We were taught to embrace the old saying, "If you want to walk fast, then walk alone, and if you want to walk far, then walk together."

Growing up in a grandfamily, embraced with the values that molded my mother, became the foundation upon which my sisters and I built our own futures. What I learned from my lived experiences, and what Donna Butts has so beautifully documented within these pages of *Grandfamilies: Stories of Children and the Loving Relatives Who Raise Them*, is that grandfamilies come in many forms. However, all have one overriding goal—to provide the buoys to keep children afloat when their parents are challenged, for whatever reason.

What then can we do, as public officials, to help grandfamilies not only survive but thrive? For one, we need to become advocates for public awareness campaigns that give grandfamilies the respect and support they deserve. According to the US Census, there are an estimated 6.7 million grandparents living with grandchildren under the age of eighteen, 2.1 million of whom are responsible for most of their basic care. In 2020, there were 6 million multigenerational US households, up from 5.1 million in 2010. If not for grandparents or other caring relatives, many or most of these children would be caught up in our already overcrowded foster care system. But grandfamilies need support beyond good wishes, as kinship caregivers are more likely to be poor, elderly, single, and unemployed. Pensions and Social Security provide fixed incomes for retirees, and adding children to the mix often sends these households into poverty.

In Maryland, forty-three thousand children are in the care of their grandparents, which is 3 percent of all children in the state. While there may be many grandparents who simply step in when their children are unable to raise their children, Maryland law allows grandparents to seek child custody, providing the legal framework for involvement in their grandchildren's lives. When this happens, it is considered formal kinship care and therefore grandparents or other relatives can apply for a bevy of supports.

Maryland is also one of only a few states that has expanded the pool of kinship foster care options to include not just grandparents or relatives but also people who have emotional connections with kids, such as family friends or coaches.

Maryland has achieved meaningful progress in supporting grandfamilies, yet we recognize there is still more work to be done. My own family's strength and wealth of experiences stem directly from being raised within a grandfamily structure. *Grandfamilies* chronicles the groundbreaking work of Generations United and the journeys of families who overcame significant challenges and emerged victorious. When intergenerational living becomes woven more deeply into America's social fabric, it will strengthen our communities, states, and the nation as a whole.

What You Can Do to Help

"I didn't say, 'Let me go find some kids to get me up at five in the morning,'" said Kathy Coleman of Louisiana's Grandparents Raising Grandchildren Information Center. The grandmother who is raising six grandchildren continued, "We didn't ask for it, but you know what? We step up. Suck it up, buttercup: We're going to raise these babies."

There are many ways you can step up to support grandfamilies in your community and nationwide. Personal connections can make a huge difference. "We all encounter shock, isolation, and loneliness," said Robyn Wind. "Just a simple phone call from *anyone* sympathetic would have been wonderful."

Grandfamilies do what they have to do—but, as Sarah Smalls said when closing her White House testimony, "We could use a little help."

If they can stay focused on making a difference, so can we all.

To begin your exploration, whether you are in a grandfamily or would like to support grandfamilies:

- Get more information about resources in your state, territory, tribe, or community. To find a list of grandfamilies service providers and support groups near you, check out GrandFacts Fact Sheets: www.grandfamilies.org/State-Fact-Sheets.

- Reach out to the contacts and programs listed that already offer support groups for grandfamilies in your area, consider a donation, and ask how you can help. If your state has a kinship navigator program (you can find out at www.gksnetwork.org/resources/kinship-navigator-programs-around-the-united-states), contact them for information about where they see gaps that could be filled. You can also search for your local Area Agency on Aging (AAA) at www.usaging.org/eldercareloc. They may offer respite, support, and other services for grandfamilies.
- If you can't commit to an ongoing role, consider a once-a-year event such as Do Something Grand on Grandparents Day, which is observed every September on the Sunday following Labor Day. Check out www.grandparentsday.org for more ideas.
- Buy and share more books. All proceeds from *Grandfamilies* go to support Generations United's work advocating and supporting grandfamilies. Buy books for holiday gifts, birthdays, and other celebrations. You'll not only educate others, you'll help a family along the way.

Here are some specific suggestions, big and small, for you to consider as you contemplate how you can assist and honor grandfamilies.

Support the Families Directly

- Organize a baby/child shower for a new grandfamily. They often don't have time to plan before the children arrive and don't have items like car seats, diapers, clothing, toys, school supplies, and so much more.
- Deliver food. School breakfast and lunch programs may take a break during the summer, holidays, and other school closures. The children are left without access to the meals they need. You can deliver groceries or a prepared meal to their home or through a support group or place of worship. Check with your local food bank and school lunch program to see what is or isn't available in your community.
- Help with childcare. Grandparents and other relatives raising children who attend support groups usually need to bring their children with them. Offer to help provide on-site childcare, activities—both fun and educational—or food during a support group meeting. There may also be a need for transportation to and from the meeting.
- During the holidays, contribute toys and gift cards. A support group may know the children's birthdays and what's on their wish list. Let the grand be the one to put the gift under the tree or give the child the gift on their special day.
- Hire a housekeeper to clean a grandfamily's home once or once a month or help with daily chores. Tackle their yard work by mowing the lawn, weeding the garden, or deadheading flowers.
- Drive a family or pay for an Uber or cab to get them to and from doctors and other appointments. If the

children are young, go inside with the family and stay with the children when the appointment is for the caregiver.

Support Education

- Contribute to or organize a back-to-school backpack drive. Local service groups, agencies, and, in some cases, fire departments conduct these before school begins to provide backpacks and school supplies for children who need them.
- Tutor a child or adolescent. Education has evolved, and grands may not have set foot in a school in years. They may not have access to technology or be up on their reading or math skills. Your tutoring time may also give a grand a break, so they can take care of business or simply rest.
- Attend a graduation; host or provide supplies for a graduation party. Cheer for the family's accomplishments.
- Give to or establish a scholarship fund that supports young people raised in grandfamilies so they can continue their education in a trade school or at a community or four-year college. For example, the Alex Smith Foundation provides older adult mentors and financial support to help put foster kids, including kinship foster kids, through college.
- Buy new back-to-school clothes or uniforms for the children. Unless it's a uniform, be sure the clothes and shoes are what the children will wear, and the grands will approve.

Support Health and Wellness

- Sponsor or lead exercise and wellness classes. Purchase a youth pass to a recreation center and give a caregiver a bit of respite. Or help a grand like Gail Engle, who said, "I couldn't teach him [her grandson] to ride a bike—I've had two knee replacements."
- Lead a cooking class featuring healthy food. Give out single recipes or create a simple cookbook. Dishes that can be prepared by both generations can be especially helpful and promote family bonding.
- Put together and deliver "self-care" gift bags to support group members. These may include body lotions, journals, or a gift certificate for a manicure.
- Provide a massage therapist to offer shoulder massages during, before, or after a support group meeting.
- Organize and lead an intergenerational grandfamily choir.
- Fulfill a dream. It could mean a trip to a local amusement park, horseback riding lessons, or a used musical instrument. Ask a support group facilitator or someone close to a family what their dreams are to see if you can help.

Support Policy Changes and Advocacy

- Advocate with your state and federal policymakers. Sign up at www.gu.org to receive policy alerts that include messages you can share when critical issues are under consideration or attack. Find out who provides the same information in your state for state policies.
- Become a Court Appointed Special Advocate (CASA) for a child in the care of a relative: https://

nationalcasagal.org/. These are trained volunteers who are assigned by a judge to advocate for the best interest of a child or youth who has been abused or neglected. CASAs support children as they prepare for court and then accompany them to hearings.

Choosing from this list of specific actions will help grandfamilies in need—some who may not even know what they need.

"I hate when someone offers to help any time, just give them a call. I tell them I could use their help with a specific thing, and they always seem to bow out," said Gail Engel. "So, I now put a list of things I need help with on my refrigerator. When someone comes to visit and offers to help, I point out the list and tell them to choose the one they would like to take on. It kind of puts them on the spot."

She continues, "A kind offering from a neighbor is only as good as the task well done and a blessing that I will cherish."

Grandfamilies have proven that they can raise children successfully. They deserve respect and a little help. The needs are great; the opportunities are limitless. It's your turn to step up.

Policy Accomplishments and Significant Events

GRANDFAMILIES & KINSHIP SUPPORT NETWORK
A National Technical Assistance Center

THIRTY YEARS OF GRANDFAMILIES POLICY ACCOMPLISHMENTS AND SIGNIFICANT EVENTS

1995-2025

Key

ABA = American Bar Association
ACL = Administration for Community Living
Brookdale = The Brookdale Foundation Group
GU = Generations United
HHS = U.S. Department of Health and Human Services
NARA = National Association for Regulatory Administration

1995
White House Conference on Aging issues Resolution 39 for grandparents raising grandchildren

1996
Federal preference for placing children with relatives over non-relatives when determining foster care placements, enacted as part of the Personal Responsibility and Work Opportunity Act

Brookdale begins their Relatives As Parents Program (RAPP)

1997
GU hosts first National Symposium on Grandparents and Other Relatives Raising Children

1998
National Kinship Care Advisory Panel begins work, with Donna Butts as member appointed by HHS Secretary

Grandfamilies House in Dorchester, MA opens as first housing specifically for grandparents raising grandchildren

1999
GU's National Center on Grandfamilies launches

2000
GU successfully advocates for relatives raising children to be included in the National Family Caregiver Support Program (NFCSP)

U.S. Census includes questions about grandparents raising grandchildren for the first time

2001
GU drafts inclusive definition of "parents" for Elementary and Secondary Education Act regulations

2003
First National GrandRally at the Capitol in Washington, DC

LEGACY Act for affordable housing for grandfamilies becomes law

2005
GU researches and adopts the term "grandfamilies" to include families in which grandparents, other relatives, or close family friends are raising children whose parents are unable to

2006
NFCSP service eligibility age lowered from 60 to 55, after GU advocacy

2007
www.grandfamilies.org established by ABA Center on Children and the Law and GU, with support from Casey Family Programs

2008

National GrandRally

Fostering Connections to Success and Increasing Adoptions Act becomes law, requiring states to identify and notify relatives when a child goes into foster care and allowing states to implement Guardianship Assistance Programs (GAP) for children to exit foster care with their kin caregivers

2014

GU releases first annual State of Grandfamilies Report

GU establishes GRAND Voices, a national group of caregiver advocates

Preventing Sex Trafficking and Strengthening Families Act is enacted, enhancing GAP

First comprehensive set of Model Family Foster Home Licensing Standards released by NARA, GU, and ABA

2016

State of Grandfamilies Report focuses on opioid epidemic

2017

60 Minutes segment on opioid epidemic and grandfamilies

U.S. Senate Finance Committee holds hearing on opioid epidemic and grandfamilies

National GrandRally

2018

Family First Prevention Services Act (FFPSA) becomes law, providing ongoing federal support for evidence-based kinship navigator programs and other prevention services for parents/kin caregivers/children

2018

$20 million appropriated to develop, enhance, or evaluate kinship navigator programs ($20 million continues to be appropriated each year through 2024, $10 million in 2025 and 2026)

Supporting Grandparents Raising Grandchildren Act creates federal advisory council on the families

2019

HHS "relies heavily" on the NARA, GU, and ABA Model as the "main source" for a National Model on Foster Family Home Licensing Standards, as required by FFPSA

2021

First and only national technical assistance center on kinship/grandfamilies - the Grandfamilies & Kinship Support Network - launches at GU, run in cooperation with ACL

2022

National Strategy to Support Family Caregivers specifically includes kinship/grandfamilies

2023

United Nations (UN) Department of Economic and Social Affairs and GU host expert symposium on families, including kinship/grandfamilies; findings included in UN General Assembly Report

Final rule allowing for separate foster care licensing standards for relatives/kin and requiring same level of support for children placed with relatives/kin and non-kin in foster care

National kin-specific foster care approval standards released from national partners, including GU

2024-25

Over 15 states and tribes implement kin-specific foster care licensing standards, with more in process

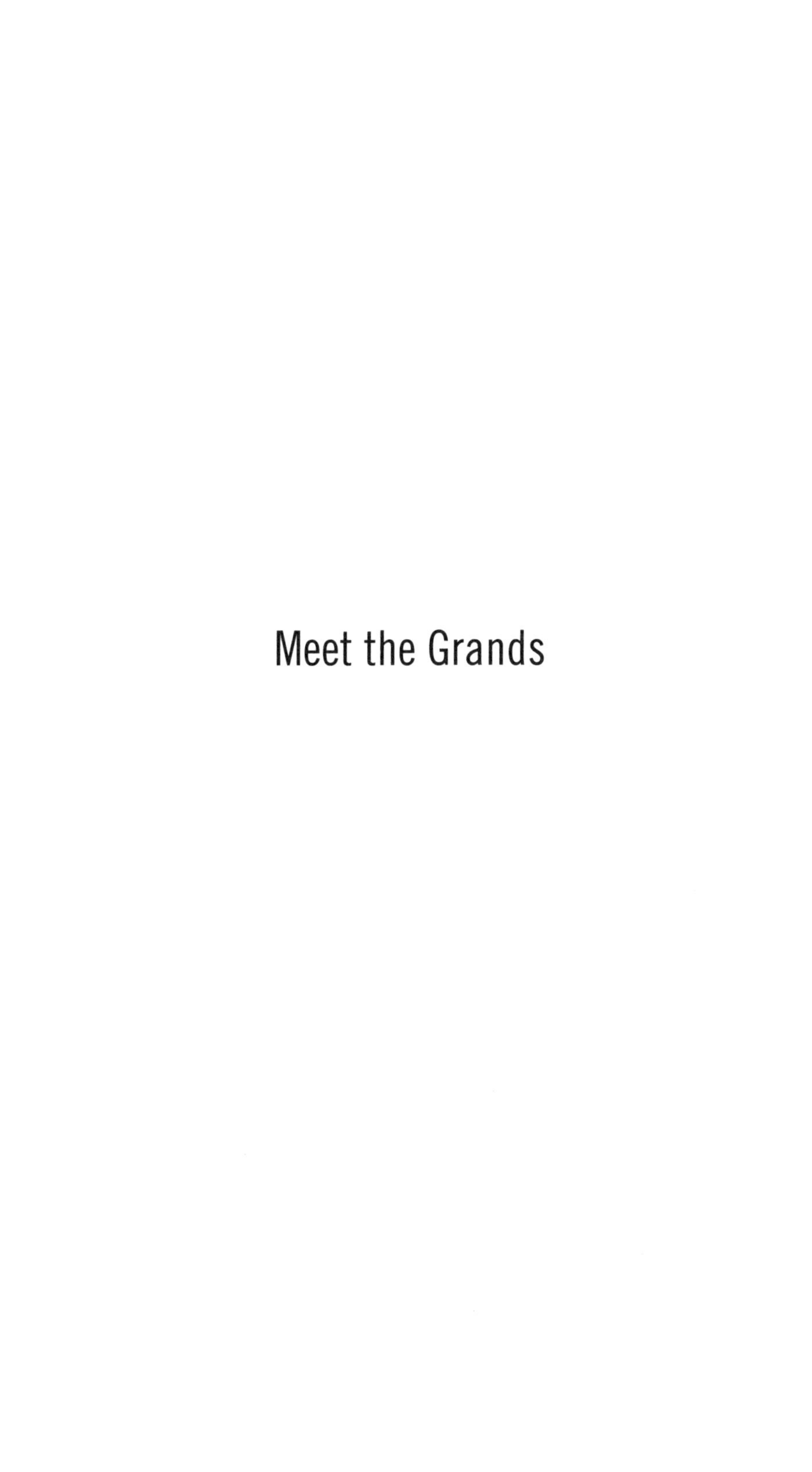

Meet the Grands

NAME	LOCATION	GRAND RELATIONSHIP
Adam Otto	West Virginia & Washington, D.C.	Grandson of **Annie & Jack Otto**
Adrian Charniak	Illinois	Grandmother to **Joey**; Married to **Ron**
Ali Siegmund	Maryland	Sister to twins, **Hannah** and **Sarah**
Alice Carter	Wyoming, Sioux	Grandmother
Annette Saunders	Maryland	Grandmother
Annie & Jack Otto	West Virginia	Grandparents to **Adam Otto**
Bob Ruble	California	Uncle
Brittney Barros	Michigan	Grandchild
Chad Dingle	Oregon	Grandchild of **Joan Dingle**
Constance Jones	Washington, D.C.	Grandmother to **Keonte Jones**
Dorothy Jenkins	New York	Grandmother
Eugene Vickerson	Georgia	Grandfather
Gail Engel	Colorado	Grandmother
Jackie Chong	Hawaii	Grandmother
Jan Wagner	Michigan	Grandmother to **Nessa**
Jaylan Gray	Texas	Sibling
Jesse Williams		Great Grandmother to **Dorese**
JJ Hitch	Michigan	Grandchild
Joan Dingle	Oregon	Grandmother to **Chad Dingle**
Keith Lowhorne	Alabama	Grandfather

NAME	LOCATION	GRAND RELATIONSHIP
Keonte Jones	Washington, D.C.	Grandchild to **Constance Jones**
Lance Robertson	Oklahoma	Grandchild
Linda Lewis	Oklahoma	Great Grandmother
Mercedes Bristol	Texas	Grandmother
Michelle Singletary	Maryland	Grandchild
Morrisella Middleton	Maryland	Grandmother
Nafeis Robinson	Pennsylvania	Brother caring for three siblings
Nickole Collins-Pierre	Illinois	Grandchild
Nikki Johnston Hurst	Pennsylvania	Grandchild
Olivia Chase	Washington, D.C.	Grandmother to **Richard**
Pat Owens	Maryland	Grandmother to **Michael**
Robert Brown	Louisiana	Grandfather
Robyn Wind	Oklahoma	Grandmother to **Jack**
Sarah Smalls	Virginia	Grandmother
Shaheed Morris	New Jersey	Grandchild
Sixto Cancel	Washington, D.C.	Foster child
Sonya Begay	Maryland	Grandmother
Stacey Walker	Iowa	Grandchild
Victoria Gray	Arizona	Grandmother
Wes Moore	Maryland	Grandchild

Endnotes

Introduction

1. "Children in Kinship Care in the United States, 2022–2024," The Annie E. Casey Foundation, datacenter.aecf.org/data/tables/10455-children-in-kinship-care?loc=1&loct=1#detailed/1/any/false/2638,2554,2479,2097,1985,1757/any/20160,20161.

Chapter One

1. "Raising the Children of the Opioid Epidemic: Solutions and Support for Grandfamilies," Generations United, 2018, 2, www.gu.org/app/uploads/2018/09/Grandfamilies-Report-SOGF-Updated.pdf.
2. Margaret Mead, *Culture and Commitment: A Study of the Generation Gap* (Natural History Press, 1970).
3. Michaeleen Doucleff, "Secrets Of Breast-Feeding From Global Moms In The Know," June 26, 2017, in *Morning Edition*, produced by NPR, www.npr.org/sections/goatsandsoda/2017/06/26/534021439/secrets-of-breast-feeding-from-global-moms-in-the-know.
4. "Family Matters: Multigenerational Living Is on the Rise and Here to Stay," Generations United, 2021, 6, www.gu.org/app/uploads/2021/04/21-MG-Family-Report-WEB.pdf.

5. "Expenditures on Children by Families 2000 Annual Report," United States Department of Agriculture Center for Policy and Promotion, 2000, fns-prod.azureedge.us/sites/default/files/expenditures_on_children_by_families/crc2000.pdf.

Chapter Two

1. "2023 State of Grandfamilies Report—Building Resilience: Supporting Grandfamilies' Mental Health and Wellness," Generations United, 2023, www.gu.org/app/uploads/2023/11/GU_2023-Grandfamilies-FullReport-FINAL.pdf.

2. "Grand Resource: Help for Grandfamilies Impacted by Opioids and Other Substance Use," Generations United, 2019, www.gu.org/resources/grand-resource-help-for-grandfamilies-impacted-by-opioids-and-other-substance-use/.

3. "Children: The Hidden Pandemic," Global Reference Group on Children Affected by COVID-19: Joint Estimates and Action, September 2022, www.spi.ox.ac.uk/files/hidden_pandemic_report_september_2022_update_pdf.

4. "Engaging Kinship Caregivers: Managing Risk Factors in Kinship Care," The Annie E. Casey Foundation, Fall 2017, assets.aecf.org/m/blogdoc/aecf-engagingkinshipcaregivers discussionguide-2017.pdf.

5. Richard Schulz and Scott R. Beach, "Caregiving as a Risk Factor for Mortality: The Caregiver Health Effects Study," *Journal of the American Medical Association* 282, no. 23 (1999): 2215–2219, doi.org/10.1001/jama.282.23.2215.

6. Joe O'Leary, interview by Colleen Pritoni, recorded June 11, 2020, StoryCorps, archive.storycorps.org/interviews/joe-oleary-and-colleen-pritoni/.

7. "Grand Resource: Help for Grandfamilies Impacted by Opioids and Other Substance Use," 5.

8. Lenora Poe, *Black Grandparents as Parents* (Lenora Madison Poe, 1992), 48.
9. Kerry Littlewood et al., "GRG tools we can use: Findings and psychometrics on the GrOW survey for grandfamily support groups," *Journal of Human Behavior in the Social Environment* 34, no. 8 (2024): 1398–1415, doi.org/10.1080/10911359.2023.2281967.
10. Soohyoung R. Lee, "Coresidence of Older Parents and Adult Children Benefits Older Adults' Psychological Well-Being: Path Analysis," *Innovation in Aging* 3, Suppl. 1 (2019): S324, doi.org/10.1093/geroni/igz038.1181.

Chapter Three

1. "Grand Resource: Help for Grandfamilies Impacted by Opioids and Other Substance Use," Generations United, 2019, www.gu.org/app/uploads/2019/01/Grandfamilies-Report-GRANDResource-Opioids.pdf.
2. "Trauma and Violence," Substance Abuse and Mental Health Services Administration, US Department of Health and Human Services, 2024, www.samhsa.gov/mental-health/trauma-violence.
3. Yanfeng Xu et al., "The Negative Effects of Adverse Childhood Experiences (ACEs) on Behavioral Problems of Children in Kinship Care: The Protective Role of Kinship Caregivers' Mental Health," *Journal of Emotional and Behavioral Disorders* 31, no. 1 (2022): 41–53, doi.org/10.1177/10634266221076475.
4. Laura Lander, Janie Howsare, and Marilyn Byrne, "The Impact of Substance Use Disorders on Families and Children: From Theory to Practice," *Social Work in Public Health* 28 (3–4) (2013): 194–205, doi:10.1080/19371918.2013.759005.

5. "'Kill the Indian in him, and save the man': R. H. Pratt on the Education of Native Americans," Carlisle Indian School Digital Resource Center, carlisleindian.dickinson.edu/teach/kill-indian-him-and-save-man-r-h-pratt-education-native-americans.
6. Robyn Wind-Tiger, "Episode 13: Robyn Wind-Tiger on the Crises Impacted Native American Grandfamilies," interview by Donna Butts, *Generations United Podcast*, produced by Generations United, July 9, 2020, www.buzzsprout.com/288531/episodes/4506536-episode-13-robyn-wind-tiger-on-the-crises-impacted-native-american-grandfamilies.
7. Emily Gold Boutilier, "How Tammy Baldwin Wins in a Divided America," *Smith Quarterly*, April 18, 2025, www.smith.edu/news-events/news/how-tammy-baldwin-wins-divided-america.
8. Tammy Baldwin, "Democratic National Convention Remarks as Prepared for Delivery," transcript of speech delivered at 2024 Democratic National Convention, Chicago, IL, August 22, 2024, https://demconvention.com/wp-content/uploads/2024/08/Prepared_Remarks_TBaldwin_0822.pdf.
9. "What Is Respite?" ARCH National Respite Network and Resource Center, archrespite.org/.
10. "Grandparents and Other Relatives Raising Children: The Second Intergenerational Action Agenda," Generations United (Washington DC, 2004).

Chapter Four

1. Simon Sandh, Vernisa M. Donaldson, and Colleen C. Katz, "Students connected to foster care: An overview of high school experiences," *Children and Youth Services Review* 113 (2020): Article 104905, doi.org/10.1016/j.childyouth.2020.104905.

2. "2024 State of Grandfamilies Report—Pathways to Success: K-12 Education Support for Kinship and Grandfamilies," Generations United, 2024, 23, www.gu.org/app/uploads/2024/09/2024GrandfamiliesReport-FullReport-FINAL-WEB.pdf.

3. "Stable Placement, Stable School: Improving Education Outcomes of Children in Foster Care in Massachusetts," Massachusetts Court Improvement Program, March 2019, www.mass.gov/files/documents/2019/04/23/Educ%20Study%20Report%20printer%20Final%20March%20 2019.pdf.

4. "2023 State of Grandfamilies Report—Building Resilience: Supporting Grandfamilies' Mental Health and Wellness," Generations United, 2023, 18, www.gu.org/app/uploads/2023/11/GU_2023-Grandfamilies-FullReport-FINAL.pdf.

5. "Summary of Attendance: Maryland Public Schools, 2005–2006," Maryland State Department of Education, Division of Accountability and Assessment, 2006, 9, marylandpublicschools.org/about/Documents/DCAA/SSP/20052006Student/2006SummaryAttendance.pdf.

6. "2022 State of Grandfamilies Report—Together at the Table: Supporting the Nutrition, Health, and Well-Being of Grandfamilies," Generations United, 2022, www.gu.org/resources/state-of-grandfamilies-report-2022/.

7. "2024 State of Grandfamilies Report," 20.

8. Deepa Fernandes, "Grandparents reflect on the struggle—and love—of raising their grandchildren," WBUR, November 23, 2023, www.wbur.org/hereandnow/2023/11/23/grand parents-raising-grandkids.

9. Bill O'Boyle, "Casey introduces legislation to support grandparents raising grandchildren," *Times Leader*, December 17, 2023, https://www.timesleader.com/opinion/

columns/1640124/casey-introduces-legislation-to-support-grandparents-raising-grandcildren.

Chapter Five

1. "2022 State of Grandfamilies Report—Together at the Table: Supporting the Nutrition, Health, and Well-Being of Grandfamilies," Generations United, 2022, www.gu.org/resources/state-of-grandfamilies-report-2022/.

2. Gabrielle Olya, "How Much Money Do Americans Have in Their Bank Accounts in 2024?" GOBankingRates, June 27, 2024, www.gobankingrates.com/banking/banking-advice/how-much-money-do-americans-have-in-their-bank-accounts-in-2024/?utm_term=related_link_3&utm_source=apple_news&utm_medium=plugin&utm_campaign=1286947&utm_content=5.

3. S. Kathi Brown, "AARP Financial Security Trends Survey, January 2025," AARP Research, May 6, 2025, doi.org/10.26419/res.00525.049.

4. Nancy Ochieng et al., "How Many Older Adults Live in Poverty?" KFF, May 21, 2024, www.kff.org/medicare/issue-brief/how-many-older-adults-live-in-poverty/.

5. Pamela Chan and Jaia Peterson Lent, "The Resounding Resiliency of Grandfamilies: Financial Stories from Older Relatives Caring for Children in Lower-Income Communities," Generations United, September 2015, www.gu.org/app/uploads/2018/05/Grandfamilies-Report-CFED-ResoundingResilienceofGrandfamilies.pdf.

6. US Census Bureau, "Grandparents," American Community Survey 1-Year Estimates Subject Tables, Table S1002, 2023, data.census.gov/table/ACSST1Y2023.S1002?q=S1002; US Census Bureau, "Poverty Status in the Last 12 Months," American Community Survey 1-Year

Estimates Subject Tables, Table S1701, 2023, data.census.gov/table/ACSST1Y2023.S1701?q=S1701.

7. Sonya Anne Begay, interview by Kayle Nanah Eppele, recorded June 11, 2020, StoryCorps, archive.storycorps.org/interviews/sonya-begay-and-kayle-eppele/.

8. Chan and Lent, "Resounding Resiliency of Grandfamilies."

9. Chan and Lent, "Resounding Resiliency of Grandfamilies," 9.

10. 42 U.S.C. § 3030s-Definitions, 2000, 1475, www.govinfo.gov/content/pkg/USCODE-2015-title42/pdf/USCODE-2015-title42-chap35-subchapIII-partE-subparti-sec3030s.pdf.

11. "National Family Caregiver Support Program," www.grandfamilies.org/Topic-Library/National-Family-Caregiver-Support-Program.

12. "2022 State of Grandfamilies Report," 19.

13. "The State of Grandfamilies in America: 2015," Generations United, 2015, 11, www.gu.org/app/uploads/2018/05/Grandfamilies-Report-SOGF-2015.pdf.

14. Jennifer Ehrle and Rob Geen, "Children Cared for by Relatives: What Services Do They Need?" The Urban Institute, June 2002, www.urban.org/sites/default/files/publication/60156/310511-Children-Cared-for-by-Relatives.PDF.

15. Maggie Davis, "It Costs an Additional $297,674 to Raise a Child Over 18 Years, Up 25.3%," LendingTree, March 13, 2025, www.lendingtree.com/debt-consolidation/raising-a-child-study/.

16. "Grand Resources: A Fact Sheet for Grandparent and Relative Caregivers to Help Access Support through the Temporary Assistance for Needy Families (TANF) Program," Generations United, 2013, www.gu.org/app/uploads/2023/04/GU-TANF-Resource.pdf.

17. "Uneven Support for Kinship/Grandfamilies: State TANF Child-Only Grants," Generations United, 2025, www.gksnetwork.org/resources/state-tanf-data/.

18. Kathleen Romig, "Social Security Lifts More People Above the Poverty Line Than Any Other Program," Center on Budget and Policy Priorities, January 21, 2025, www.cbpp.org/research/social-security/social-security-lifts-more-people-above-the-poverty-line-than-any-other#_ftn2.
19. "Fact Sheet: The Benefits of Social Security for Grandfamilies," Generations United, 2010, www.gu.org/app/uploads/2019/03/Grandfamilies-Report-BenefitsofSocial-SecurityforGrandfamilies.pdf.
20. Matthew P. Rabbitt, Laura J. Hales, and Madeline Reed-Jones, "Food Security in the U.S.–Measurement," United States Department of Agriculture Economic Research Service, January 8, 2025, www.ers.usda.gov/topics/food-nutrition-assistance/food-security-in-the-us/measurement.
21. "2022 State of Grandfamilies Report," Generations United.
22. "2022 State of Grandfamilies Report," Generations United.
23. "2022 State of Grandfamilies Report," Generations United.
24. US Census Bureau, "Smithville, Tennessee," Quick-Facts, www.census.gov/quickfacts/fact/table/smithvillecity tennessee/HSG445223.

Chapter Six

1. "2019 State of Grandfamilies Report—A Place to Call Home: Building Affordable Housing for Grandfamilies," Generations United, 2019, www.gu.org/app/uploads/2019/11/19-Grandfamilies-Report-APlacetoCallHome.pdf.
2. "How many households in the United States spend too much on housing?" USA Facts, 2025, usafacts.org/answers/how-many-households-in-the-united-states-spend-too-much-on-housing/country/united-states/.
3. "2019 State of Grandfamilies Report," Generations United.

4. Alison S. Gottleib et al., "Life at GrandFamilies House: The First Six Months," *Gerontology Institute Publications*, 2000, scholarworks.umb.edu/cgi/viewcontent.cgi?article=1022&context=gerontologyinstitute_pubs.
5. Dorothy Jenkins and Donna Butts, "Raising Grandchildren in Communities of Color," interview by Ed Gordon, *News & Notes* podcast, produced by NPR, November 1, 2005, www.npr.org/2005/11/01/4984113/raising-grandchildren-in-communities-of-color.
6. *Legacy*, directed by Tod Lending (2000, PBS: Public Broadcasting Service).
7. Cathy Free, "A contractor stole their money. The community rallied to fix their flooded home," *The Washington Post*, August 23, 2022, www.washingtonpost.com/lifestyle/2022/08/23/home-renovated-for-two-brothers/.

Epilogue

1. "What Happens to Youth Aging Out of Foster Care?" Annie E. Casey Foundation, February 25, 2025, www.aecf.org/blog/what-happens-to-youth-aging-out-of-foster-care.
2. "Kinship/Grandfamilies Data," Grandfamilies and Kinship Support Network, Generations United, May 2025, www.gksnetwork.org/kinship-data/.
3. Sixto Cancel, "A Brief But Spectacular take on prioritizing kinship care," *PBS News Hour*, May 31, 2023, www.pbs.org/newshour/brief/447461/sixto-cancel.
4. 42 U.S. Code § 627 – Family Connection Grants, 2014, 18, www.govinfo.gov/content/pkg/USCODE-2013-title42/pdf/USCODE-2013-title42-chap7-subchapIV-partB-subpart1-sec627.pdf.
5. "The Family First Prevention Services Act: Successes, Road Blocks, and Opportunities for Improvement, Before

the United States Senate Finance Committee, 117th Cong." (May 2024), written testimony of Laurie Tapozada (kinship caregiver, peer mentor, and kinship navigator professional), www.finance.senate.gov/imo/media/doc/05222024_tapozada_testimony.pdf.

Acknowledgments

Acknowledgments often list family last. That doesn't seem right for a book about family—whether related by blood or love or both. So I start with my heart.

To my husband and best friend, Bill Libro. You make me stop, even when I'm soooo busy, to look at a sunset I'll never see again, watch fireflies dancing during their short lives, and take in a rainbow that could disappear in seconds. You make me pause, breathe, and remember to be grateful. And I will always be grateful for you.

To my family of origin and family of choice—you know who you are. You make birthdays, holidays, and every day a celebration. We've been there for each other and always will be . . . despite some of your quirks. Not mine.

To team Generations United—the board, staff, partners, and funders. You've lived and breathed this work and continue to do it together. You know that it's never been about me but always about we. I never could have known more than twenty-five years ago that my life would be blessed with a leadership trifecta—Ana Beltran, Jaia Peterson Lent, and Sheri Steinig. I'm in awe of your brilliance and dedication to our mission. As a lovely African gentleman told a friend of mine years ago, your heart is as big as your body. The world is better because of you.

To Adrian Charniak and all the GRANDs and Grand Successes who shared their stories in hopes of others seeing grandfamilies with a more compassionate lens. You are courageous, an inspiration and my heroes.

To my writing team—editor and coach Sarah J. Robbins, who carried me through challenging times and challenged me in others, and Ellie Van Houten, research assistant extraordinaire.

To the Brookdale Foundation staff, especially Mary Ann Van Clief, for making an early investment in this book. You made it possible to go from an idea to an "OMG, what have I gotten myself into?" Thank you.

The posse that encouraged, chided, and guided me along the way—Marci Alboher, Mary Bissell, Jeremy Blachman, Bob Blancato, Allison Burchell, Joo Yeun Chang, Joe Cuticelli, Marc Freedman, Sarah Gesiriech, Marlene Goldman, Ellen Goldstein, Amy Goyer, Gerri Mason Hall, Margaret Mark, Joy Thomas Moore, Micheal Morris, Barbara Pryor, John Rother, Derenda Schubert, Michelle Singletary, Mackenzie Smith, Pam Smith, Julie Tippens, Marvin Waldman, Stefanie Weiss, Juan Williams, and Marcia Withers.

To the policymakers, partners, and advocates whose commitment to making a difference for the families proved impactful: Senators Tammy Baldwin, Sherrod Brown, Bob Casey, Hillary Clinton, Susan Collins, Mike DeWine, Charles Grassley, Orrin Hatch, Patty Murray, Jay Rockefeller, Olympia Snowe, Debbie Stabenow, and Ron Wyden. Representatives Karen Bass, Mike Capuano, Danny Davis, Jim McGovern, and Connie Morella. Advocates and partners Heidi Redlich Epstein, Rob Geen, Melinda Perez Porter, and Linda Spears.

To She Writes Press/Stable Book Group for giving me the path to publish and to Simon & Schuster for distributing the book.

Finally, thanks to you, the reader, who I hope will look at grandfamilies differently and reach out to them with respect, appreciation, and support.

About the Author

Author photo © Ginny Filer Photography

Donna Butts is an award-winning nonprofit executive, author, and trusted voice frequently quoted in the national media. As executive director of Generations United, a role she served in for more than twenty-seven years, she was invited to testify before Congress, address the United Nations, speak before the Federal Reserve Board, and present in more than a dozen countries, including at the World Human Rights Cities Forum in South Korea. She blogged for the Huffington Post for four years, covering intergenerational relations, grandfamilies, and health. Her writing also has appeared in several books and more than a dozen publications. Appointed in 1998 to the first Kinship Care Advisory Panel by then–Department of Health and Human Services Secretary Donna Shalala, Donna has helped pave the way for crucial legislation and support for grandfamilies. She has been a part of eight United Nations expert group meetings on intergenerational solidarity and dialogue, focusing on the changing demographics and the value of older adults.

For more information about Donna and *Grandfamilies*, please visit **www.donnambutts.com**.

Looking for your next great read?

We can help!

Visit www.shewritespress.com/next-read
or scan the QR code below for a list
of our recommended titles.

She Writes Press is an award-winning
independent publishing company founded to
serve women writers everywhere.